// LEGAL ISSUES JOURNAL
Volume 7, Issue 2
July 2019

Legal Issues Journal (LIJ) publishes original research on all legal matters affecting justice, equality and other pressing issues for societies. The journal welcomes interdisciplinary work at the intersection of law and other disciplines, such as genetics, biosciences, philosophy, linguistics, neuroscience, medicine, and business.

The Journal publishes original papers, case comments, short reports, debates and book reviews. The Journal also provides important news and interpretation on changes in the legal world and coming trends affecting law, lawyers, and society. Contribution to society, nationally and internationally, is the focus of LIJ.

LIJ uses double-blind peer review process – both the reviewer(s) and the author(s) are anonymous.

ISSN 2516-1210 (Print)
ISSN 2515-9887 (Online)

The United Kingdom Law and Society Association

Table of Contents

A Note from the Executive Publisher

Legal Issues Journal widens its scope to include an inter-disciplinary dimension – building bridges between law and science

Legal journals play a vital role in supporting and promoting justice. Many legal journals focus on single disciplines. However, as science progresses, we accumulate knowledge from different disciplines that is relevant to explaining faults in the justice process. For example, genetic science enabled us to find out that justice systems wrongly convicted a large number of people. Moreover, psychology and neuroscience have generated much insights into the sources of wrongful convictions and other justice flaws, such as memory faults and attentional and other biases.

Genetic science and neuroscience findings are also showing that many elements of the justice process are based on incorrect understanding of human behaviour and capability. For example, research has shown that human behaviour is a product of complex gene-environment processes, and that individual differences in behaviour and thought have a complex, multi-factorial nature. Moreover, advancements in genetics are enabling probabilistic prediction of different traits from information stored in our DNA.

Findings also show that our ability to tell whether someone is lying or telling the truth is very poor, that decision-making is largely unconscious and influenced by many factors, and that traits are a continuum, for example there is no clear line between what we call normal and abnormal.

To recognise the significance of interdisciplinary work and collaboration for justice, LIJ has widened its scope to include an interdisciplinary dimension. Our recent publications include interdisciplinary papers, such as genetics and human rights (see *Genetic Data Misuse: Risk to Fundamental Human Rights in Developed Economies*). By publishing interdisciplinary work, we aim to encourage inter-disciplinary collaborations between lawyers and experts from other disciplines – to build bridges between science and the law.

In addition to legal research, LIJ invites original interdisciplinary research on a range of legal matters affecting society, such as legal and ethical aspects of genetics, neuroscience and bioethics. The Journal publishes original papers, case comments, short reports, debates and book reviews. LIJ also provides important news and interpretation on changes in the legal world and coming trends affecting law, lawyers, and society.

LIJ is fully administered by pro-bono contributions of an international team of researchers and practitioners, scientists and lawyers – who share a common interest of contributing to justice. The Journal uses double-blind peer review process. Both the reviewer(s) and the author(s) are anonymous. The Journal provides fast online publication, and we welcome proposals for special issues.

Fatos Selita
Executive Publisher

Is there a Justification for the Existence of Patent Law in the International Pharmaceutical Industry?

Bashayer Al-Mukhaizeem[1]

University of Sussex

Summary. Moral and economic dilemmas are often caused by the patent system as new drugs enter the market. This is because patents are mostly centred on economic profit, regardless of the possible negative consequences on public health.[2] Some of the consequences include the difficulty for the less economically-advantaged classes to access particular drugs[3] and that a drug is often isolated from competition as a result of a 20-year mandated monopoly. Competition would contribute to a proliferation of medical products and, therefore, reduce the holistic medication price.[4] Access to effective and affordable medicines is regarded as a prerequisite for global public health. At the same time, the pharmaceutical industries deserved remuneration for the product and its value which they produce. The current system is flawed and must be restructured.

1. Introduction

Patentability, under the Agreement on Trade-related Aspects (TRIPS), is the protection given to novel inventions.[5] This protection is presented through the monopoly of the creative item, having an exclusive right to be manufactured only by the inventor in return for disclosing novel in-

[1] Email: bosha_mhd@yahoo.com.

[2] Muzaka (n 6) 156.

[3] Yvette Madrid ; Germán Velásquez & Enrique Fefer, 'The Economics of Pharmaceuticals and Health Sector Reform in the Americas' (1998) 3(5) Revista Panamericana de Salud Pública 343.

[4] *Ibid* 344.

[5] The Agreement on Trade-related Aspects of Intellectual property Rights 1994 (TRIPS) Article 27(1).

formation.[6] According to the TRIPS,[7] this right lasts for twenty years from the date of registering a patent, and within this period, other companies are excluded from exploiting the invention.[8] Many bilateral and multilateral pharmaceutical trade and investment agreements follow the same strategy of long-term monopolisation of patents.[9] Moreover, some of them have stricter rules than TRIPS, especially with regards to the extensions of exclusivity.[10] The pharmaceutical patent-period was considerably shorter before TRIPS influenced the industry.[11]

Advocates of the patent system have explained its benefits:[12] they argue that the patent system incentivises inventors to publish and circulate their beneficial information.[13] However, some items, such as some drugs, are excluded from patentability in case of extraordinary necessity in protecting public health.[14]

In this article, I will assess the patent system as an incentive for further research. Then, I will examine the impact of patents on the market, and the impact of patents on developing countries. Following that, I will highlight how it may be possible to strike a balance between human rights and patents on one hand, and patents and generics on the other. Finally, I will evaluate the suitability of patents to be applied over pharmaceuticals and I will propose alternatives to the patent system, as we shall see.

2. Patents as an Incentive for Research

Biomedical processes are undeniably expensive and protracted.[15] Alan Devlin, for instance, has argued that, in the absence of exclusive rights,

---

[6] Lionel Bently & Brad Sherman, *Intellectual Property Law* (Oxford, Oxford University Press 2014) 357.

[7] TRIPS Article 33.

[8] Bently & Sherman (n 2) 375.

[9] Valbona Muzaka, 'Prizes for Pharmaceuticals? Mitigating the Social ineffectiveness of the current Pharmaceutical Patent Arrangement' (2013) 34(1) Third World Quarterly 151.

[10] Rory Horner, 'The Impact of Patents on Innovation, Technology Transfer and Health: A Pre- and Post-Trips Analysis of India's Pharmaceutical Industry' (2014) 19(3) New Political Economy 384, 399.

[11] Muzaka (n 6) 154.

[12] Bently & Sherman (n 2) 379.

[13] *Ibid* 379.

[14] TRIPS Article 27(2).

[15] Reaches nine years, Alan Devlin, 'Systemic Bias in Patent Law' (2012) 61 DePaul Law Review 57, 67.

pharmaceutically high-priced experimentation would deteriorate significantly.[16] Rightly, many research projects are long and cost millions of dollars, but do not always make a proportionate contribution to science.[17] Highly-priced patented medicines may provide only a small benefit over existing ones.[18] Furthermore, the patent system may actually reduce the efficiency of the product instead of promoting and contributing to the production of effective medication. The 'first-come-first-serve policy' that underlies the patent system, or what is called 'first-to-file', contributes to the unworkability and underdevelopment of drugs, as manufacturers work under the influence of time pressure in order to gain the monopoly of a particular drug.[19] The more problematic aspect of some pieces of legislation, such as The Code of Laws of the United States of America (US Code), concerns 'faulty' inventions. Under such legislation, if the invention has an error, and that error is identified within the period of two years from the date of the patent issuance, the inventor is allowed to remedy the defect. This is problematic because it gives the inventor the chance to expand the boundaries of his invention by minimising the information which was previously accessible to the public on the grounds that the inventor is invalid in its original application.[20] A further problem which arises from this approach is uncertainty regarding the drugs' benefits and patent rights, as only after the expiration of the two-year period is a drug officially fortified.[21] This corrective power could encourage patentees to accelerate the registration of their drugs, even if they are not certain of the medication's possible dangerous effects.

A pharmaceutical company seeks to protect its valuable and profitable notions through the patent system. Otherwise, the company is likely to pursue the so-called 'trade secrets' approach on the methods of medicine-manufacturing and its effective ingredients.[22] Resorting to a 'top secret' strategy would extend the commercial exploitation of pharmaceutical information for longer than the monopolistic period of a patent as long as

[16] *Ibid* 59.

[17] Richard Hosmer Blum, *Pharmaceuticals and Health Policy* (New York: Holmes & Meier Publishers 1981) 63.

[18] Elias Mossialos; Monique Mrazek & Tom Maidenhead, *Regulating Pharmaceuticals in Europe: Striving for Efficiency, Equity and Quality* (Berkshire: Open University Press 2004) 354.

[19] Jay Mattappally, 'Goliath Beats David: Undoing the Leahy-Smith America Invents Act's Harmful Effects on Small Businesses Comment' (2012) 58 Loyola Law Review 981, 1013.

[20] United States Code 2000 Title 35 para 251.

[21] Charlie Lisherness, 'Patent Reissue Genus Claims: Harmful Evolution' (2003) 26 Thomas Jefferson Law Review 85, 86 & 98.

[22] Mattappally (n 19) 1021.

it remains secret.[23] Notwithstanding, some legislations apparently encourage keeping product information confidential rather than submitting it to the patent system. For example, under the America Invents Act (AIA),[24] if company (A) alleges patent infringement by company (B) which uses a similar formula to manufacture a competitive medicine, then company (B) may counterclaim that its product commercially used the formula before the patented application of company (A)'s product, on the basis of secret protection. The effect of this defence is to refute the allegation of infringement.[25]

This clarifies that the patent system may not have a great role in stimulating pharmaceutical companies to disclose their novel information. On the other hand, the patent system can negatively contribute encouraging these companies to increase the price of drugs, which impacts the purchasing power of the market.

3. The Impact of Patent on the Market and Productivity

Pragmatically, a company with patented drugs can continue increasing its prices if there is not another drug on the market that serves the same or similar purposes. This, therefore, renders the new pharmaceutical sector inelastic.[26] Elasticity depends heavily on the 'supply' and 'demand' factors, and as long as there is no market competitor, because of the monopoly, the supply is limited. This increases prices, especially when demand for the medicine is high, and this is the case for many monopolised medicines. Medicines are essential for people who are ill, and they are indispensable, particularly if there are no alternatives. This limited access combined with relatively high prices could result in a reduction in life expectancy,[27] either because the patentee's capacity cannot meet the high demand of the medicine, or because some people cannot afford the cost of the new medication. The patent system can also affect a country's labour[28] situation, as lower-class patients may not be able to perform their work to sufficient standards due to ill health. This could have a sig-

[23] *Ibid* 1021.

[24] America Invents Act (2011) Sec. 5(a) para 273.

[25] Mattappally (n 19) 1023-1024.

[26] Dong-Churl Suh; Willard Manning; Stephen Schondelmeyer & Ronald Hadsall, "Effect of Multiple-Source Entry on Price Competition after Patent Expiration in the Pharmaceutical Industry" (2000) 35(2) Health Services Research 529, 533.

[27] Srividhya Ragavan, *Patent and Trade Disparities in Developing Countries* (Oxford: Oxford University Press 2012) 197-198

[28] *Ibid* 197-198.

nificant impact on the economic output of a State, and ultimately lead to a reduction of its productivity.[29] In 2003 and at the time of the development of a disease called Severe Acute Respiratory Syndrome (SARS), the World Health Organization (WHO) strongly recommend the postponement of any unnecessary travel to Thailand and China in order to stop the global spread of SARS, and in order to protect international public health.[30] This had a severe impact on the tourism industries of China and Thailand. [31] In 2016, it was reported that 7.1 million people in South Africa suffered from Acquired Immune Deficiency Syndrome (AIDS);[32] this dramatically affected employees as a result of the cost of medication, and affected employers and companies though an overall decline in productivity.[33] In 2005, the Brazilian government refused to allow drugs to combat AIDS to be patented in order to allow sufficient levels of medication to be produced locally.[34]

There are other detrimental repercussions of pharmacological patents on the market, including the misallocation of resources in certain companies with patents. Let us explain this point; when a company discovers a cure that effectively eliminates a deadly disease, the active substance in this drug may be prevented from being used by other companies or even by individuals because of the monopoly. Thus, the issue cannot be associated only with monopolising the medicine, but also with monopolising ingredients. Other possible negative outcome of monopolising medicines is that some countries are restricted from importing foreign-patented drugs, although the ingredients of the medicine may be available internally, industrial capacity is available and local production is feasible. This weakens market forces due to the creation of an uncompetitive environment. It also hinders innovative local research around the same disease through fear of producing a medicine possessing similar features to the patented drug. Accordingly, this results in the transferal of local funds to foreign investments, and this limited the economic growth of the local community. All of these consequences are likely to affect drugs' avail-

29 *Ibid* 197-198.

30 World Health Organization, 'Update 61 - WHO extends its SARS related travel advice to all of Taiwan province, China" (21 May 2003) <http://www.who.int/csr/don/2003_05_21a/en/> accessed 20 April 2016

31 Ragavan (n 28) 197-198.

32 Avert, "HIV And AIDS in South Africa' (2017) <https://www.avert.org/professionals/hiv-around-world/sub-saharan-africa/south-africa> accessed 20 April 2016

33 Ragavan (n 28) 197-198.

34 Ragavan (n 28) 193-194.

ability. [35] When a company fails to provide its patented medication, the drug is unavailable in the importing country and the receiving country is prohibited from producing similar products because of the monopoly.[36] Patented drugs would increase the price, even if an alternative cheaper drug is available in the international market,[37] as the stipulation of novelty for patentability is limited to the country where the patent is registered.[38]

Notably, TRIPS does not define the creative requirement of a patent, which gives some countries the flexibility to adjust this criterion according to their own socioeconomic conditions.[39] In the *KSR International Co. v. Teleflex Inc* case, the US Supreme Court[40] took into account the surrounding circumstances in order to determine patentability, not only in response to market pressure.[41] If a medicine was invented as a result of business competition, the oligopolistic price of a patent system would lead to excessive social expenditure.[42] This is on the grounds that the pharmaceutical companies would run production processes only if profitability exceeds the manufacturing costs. In this case, the yield is probably gained twice; from the market competition and from patent law. Within a short period far less than that of the patented period, it is likely that the profit gained because of the huge demand for the medicine largely surpasses the expenditure spent on research and industry. An extended patented period would substantially deprive consumers of access to alternative, cheaper drugs for a long time, especially as the generic medicine would be available if the products were patented for a shorter period. The result would be more severe if consumers are from developing countries.

---

35 Arman Kirim, 'Reconsidering Patents and Economic Development: A Case Study of the Turkish Pharmaceutical Industry' (1985) 13(2) World Development 219, 221.

36 *Ibid* 221.

37 *Ibid* 221.

38 StopFakes, 'What is a Patent?' (7 July 2016) < http://www.stopfakes.gov/learn-about-ip/patents/about> accessed 12 December 2015.

39 Janice Mueller, 'Taking TRIPS to India — Novartis, Patent Law, and Access to Medicines' (2007) 356(6) The New England Journal of Medicine 541, 543.

40 *KSR International Co. v Teleflex Inc.* (2007) 550 US 398 (US Supreme Court)

41 Laura Pedraza-Farina, 'Patent Law and the Sociology of Innovation' (2013) 2 Wisconsin Law Review 813, 815-818.

42 *Ibid* 817.

4. The Impact of Patents on Developing Countries

The price of already-expensive patented drugs is even higher in developing countries than industrial ones because of the exchange rate and transport cost.[43] Many developing countries have weak infrastructures and too low per capita incomes, and this aids the spread of disease. For instance, schistosomiasis, or bilharzia, is a neglected tropical disease (NTD) and, according to WHO, the highest rate of Schistosomiasis is found in rural areas of Africa, where nine out of ten people requiring treatment for the disease are located.[44] This kind of disease is common in a low-income population and is caused by '...a parasitic worm that lives in fresh water in subtropical and tropical regions.'[45] Many people in rural areas in Egypt, for instance, suffering from Schistosomiasis are struggling to find something to eat. Given their situation, it would not occur to them to buy a branded patented medicine. Many people in the same situation as these people would ignore their illness because they cannot afford the medicine, and this would be problematic. This causes social fracture as the unwell person would not be able to look after his or her family, support them, or provide them with their day-to-day needs etc. As a result, their offspring may behave inappropriately or illegally in the absence of domestic structure and guidance. This is in addition to the economic problems affecting the family and a lack of educational opportunities for the children. This constitutes a fundamental problem for society as a whole. In 2016, WHO showed that approximately 90 million individuals were treated for schistosomiasis due to the State and international institutions' intervention.[46]

In India, medicine prices increased roughly 42% after the enforcement of TRIPS, and consumer welfare decreased by about $9 million per medicament.[47] According to Article 30 of TRIPS:

---

43 Blum (n 17) 192.

44 World Health Organization, 'Schistosomiasis: WHO reports substantial treatment progress for school-age Children' (8 December 2017) <http://www.who.int/neglected_diseases/news/WHO_schistosomiasis_reports_substantial_treatment_progress_sac/en/> accessed 18 April 2018.

45 NHS, Schistosomiasis (bilharzia) < https://www.nhs.uk/conditions/schistosomiasis/> accessed 18 April 2018.

46 World Health Organization, (n 44).

47 Antara Dutta, 'From Free Entry to Patent Protection: Welfare Implications for the Indian Pharmaceutical Industry' (2011) 93(1) The Review of Economics and Statistics 160, 177.

> Members may provide limited exceptions to the exclusive rights conferred by a patent, provided that such exceptions do not unreasonably conflict with a normal exploitation of the patent and do not unreasonably prejudice the legitimate interests of the patent owner, taking account of the legitimate interests of third parties.

If the national law of a developing country permits making use of the patent subject matter without authorisation of the patent's right holder, the TRIPS agreement provides further conditions.[48] The apparent stipulations of the TRIPS are that such unauthorised use should be limited to the existence of a 'national emergency';[49] and the use of the patent subject-matter should be restricted 'for the supply for the domestic market'.[50] However, these conditions may not be suitable for developing countries as many of them have no capacity to manufacture anti-retroviral drugs[51] and importation in this case is not allowed under TRIPS. Indeed, the Doha Declaration on the TRIPS Agreement and Public Health requires 'compulsory licenses' in emergency cases[52] and permits the import of drugs if the country lacks the resources to manufacture.[53] The problem is that TRIPS was probably drafted to reflect the circumstances and reality of developed countries, where governments can react rapidly to the spread of an illness as an urgent matter. By contrast, in developing countries, this is a constant problem and cannot only be classified as a temporarily necessity.

Additionally, developing countries which may lack new inventions may suffer considerably from permitting patentees to export information of unpatented drugs elsewhere, as this results in expensive patented medication.[54] Moreover, some inventions of outstanding ideas from developing countries may face difficulties in applying for patents due to their expensive bureaucracy.[55] The actual beneficiaries of such a system would most probably be global commercial firms of industrial countries.[56]

---

48 TRIPS Article 31.
49 TRIPS Article 31(b).
50 TRIPS Article 31(f).
51 James Chalmers, *Legal Responses to HIV and AIDS* (Oxford: Hart Publishing 2008) 163.
52 Doha Declaration on the TRIPS Agreement and Public Health 2001 (Doha Declaration) para 5(b) & (c).
53 Doha Declaration, para 6.
54 Bently & Sherman (n 2) 379.
55 Morten Tvedt, 'One Worldwide Patent System: What's in it for Developing Countries?' (2010) 31(2) Third World Quarterly 277, 281.
56 *Ibid* 280 & 288.

Furthermore, countries with limited purchasing power will be less attractive to the international pharmaceutical firms to research on their diseases; such diseases are consequently ignored simply because the patented medicine designed to tackle them would not be profitable.[57] Additionally, the markets of many developing countries are relatively small in comparison to the international desideratum to treat a number of common diseases such as hypertension, ulcers or even cancer.[58] Thus, industrial parties have minimal interest in investing their pharmaceutical patents in poor nations. Therefore, it is unlikely that the patent system incentivises research in such countries.[59] Accordingly, medical research is unlikely to be based on diseases unique to developing nations simply because the expensive monopolised medicine will not be bought.[60] This is because the demand for medications is elastic in developing countries, depending on the price[61] rather than depending on health care. Accordingly, if the price of medication in developing countries is high, patients can endure the symptoms or use any alternatives by either using nothing and enduring the symptoms of their illness without respite, or using folk medicine, which may work for some diseases but not all of them. This contributes significantly to the spread of contagious diseases. Other patients may resort to severe alternatives, such as alcohol or drug addiction. Others may even resort to suicide. This is despite the fact that having a healthy life is regarded as the primary factor of human rights.

5. Human Rights versus Patent

Many international treaties and organisations emphasise the importance of public health, which prevails over private rights. For example, the International Covenant on Economic, Social and Cultural Rights[62] requires States to ensure the highest attainable standard of physical and mental health. The Action Programme on Essential Drugs requires States to make high-quality medicines available at reasonable prices.[63] Despite these requirements, patent regimes lead to high prices in medicines to

57 Muzaka (n 6) 156.

58 Ragavan (n 28) 36.

59 *Ibid* 36.

60 *Ibid* 195.

61 *Ibid.*

62 International Covenant on Civil and Political Rights (1966) Article 6. It also mentions that the right to life should not be arbitrarily deprived. See also: The International Covenant on Economic, Social and Cultural Rights (ICESCR) (1966) Article 12.

63 The Action Programme on Essential Drugs (1979) Article 2(1).

maximise the monopoly revenue. The high prices allow diseases to spread among the poor especially. It also encourages 'quick' manufacturing of medication, even if this may compromise the quality of the drug and its effectiveness in eradicating the illnesses. This may encourage manufacturing medicines that mitigate, but do not eradicate, the illness to ensure patients use the medicament as long as possible for the sake of profit gains.[64] The WHO requires States to promote and enhance the quality of medicines, and to reduce their side-effects.[65] However, the monopoly in pharmaceuticals patents impedes intellectual development by freezing ideas for a 20-year period. Inventors may want to improve exiting patents, in particular by strengthening their impact and by reducing possible negative side-effects. Nevertheless, they are prohibited from doing so.

Human rights conflict with the implementation of patents, as patents lead to expensive medicines and impede easy access to medicines through drug monopolisation by a single supplier. This has a severe ramification on the right to health.[66] The Universal Declaration of Human Rights (UDHR) states that everyone has the right to protect their material interest which results from scientific production.[67] However, the UDHR also emphasises that everyone has the right to enjoy a high standard of living, commensurate with good health.[68] It is not an easy task to strike a balance between these two conflicting interests; on the one hand, the interests of the community and, on the other, the interests of the creators of innovative works.

Another relevant human rights treaty is the US Declaration on the Rights of Indigenous Peoples (DRIP). This Declaration asserts indigenous people's right to control over, inter alia, the fauna and flora over such cultural heritage. The trend lies in the fact that many medicines nowadays are based on the global renaissance for the recourse to natural treatments and the relinquishment of chemical medicines with harsh side effects. This trend contributes to the transformation of research methods and subsequently methods of manufacturing medicines. Because natural ingredients such as herbs, plants and oils are not available in every country, but are concentrated in some countries, the dependence of large com-

---

64 Phoebe Li, *Health Technologies and International Intellectual Property* (London: Routledge 2014) 22.

65 World Health Organization, 'Saving Lives through the Promotion of Quality Medicines' <http://www.who.int/medicines/services/expertcommittees/pharmprep/qual_med_promo_save-lives/en/> accessed 13 December 2016.

66 Johanna Gibson, *Patenting Lives: Life Patents, Culture and Development* (Cornwall: TJ international 2008) 65-66.

67 The Universal Declaration of Human Rights (UDHR) (1948) Article 27(2).

68 UDHR Article 25(1).

panies on natural resources and ecological diversity in those countries is very substantial. This total dependence rarely pays regard to the right of the original holders to participate in the profits of pharmaceutical companies, nor to the recognition of their contributions.[69] Some biotechnological industries, however, exploit the environment and gain a lot from exclusive rights, denying disempowered source countries their rightful share of the benefits,[70] contrary to DRIP.[71] The result can be harsher if the indigenous people are not allowed to use their natural sources to produce generics fighting the same diseases that the branded patented medicine does but with low prices.

6. Patents and Generics

Through generic drugs, the cost of medication per patient is reduced from $5,000 to $365 per year in Latin America.[72] Some of the high-quality generic pharmaceuticals marketed at relatively cheap prices are produced by the Julphar Company.[73] Their affordability is attributed to the fact that the materials are imported from China, and to the fact that they are manufactured locally.[74] In 2007, the Government of Thailand decided to use compulsory licenses against patented-drugs, in order to introduce cheaper generic versions.[75] Its ultimate purpose was to tackle diseases like AIDS and blood clotting.[76] This can result in conflicting repercussions; a well-known branded drug company reduced the price of their drugs, but another company threatened to stop commercialising in Thailand.[77] The latter company argued that the patented drug company invested millions of dollars and spent years creating such medication and, unfortunately, generic-medicine producers simply duplicated the final stage of the branded-drug.[78] However, the government distributed the generic drugs only to those who were unable to pay,[79] and on the grounds

69 Gibson (n 68) 65-66.
70 *Ibid.*
71 UN Declaration on the Rights of Indigenous Peoples (2008) Article 31(1).
72 That was in 2004. Chalmers (n 52) 160.
73 The Pharma Letter, *UAE's Julphar Inks Five-year Deal to Market Merck & Co Drugs* (11 April 2014).
74 Dutta (n 48) 177.
75 Jakkrit Kuanpoth, *Patent Rights in Pharmaceuticals in Developing Countries* (Cheltenham: Edward Elgar 2010) 181-184.
76 *Ibid.*
77 Devlin (n 15) 68.
78 *Ibid.*
79 *Ibid* 68.

that the poor would not buy the patented medicine any way, even if there were not a generic version. As a result, the commercial performance of branded-drugs was not actually affected. The Office of US Trade Representative (USTR)[80] exerted pressure on Thailand not to use compulsory licenses, by revoking trade privileges under the Generalised System of Preferences (GSP).[81] It also required a limit to the application of compulsory licensing under trade agreement with Thailand;[82] and to place Thailand on the Priority Watch List (PWL), which regards that the intellectual property regime of Thailand is of concern.[83]

The patent system significantly diminishes the volume of cheaper, generic versions of patented drugs during monopoly timeframes.[84] This is particularly true when patent systems permit the expansion of the monopoly of the patent area[85] in order for it to be confined to a company for decades.[86] For example, when an antibiotic is discovered to eradicate harmful bacteria without affecting the good ones, the coverage of this specialised field may prevent newcomers from creating new drugs or generics because of the monopoly of the patented information. This is the case even if the ingredients of the patented medicine and the new one are different. This prevention could be due to the method of the remedy and to fight the bacteria is the same in both medicines. This expansion of monopolising the whole area of patented drugs, including their ingredients, the way the body absorbs them and the method to remedy the disease, would disrupt medical development and scientific research around the patented drugs.

---

[80] USTR identifies countries which do not provide effective protection of intellectual property rights. Office of the United States Trade Representative, 'Intellectual Property' <https://ustr.gov/issue-areas/intellectual-property> accessed 23 December 2015.

[81] It provides opportunities for many of the Third world's countries to trade in order to grow their economies. Office of the United States Trade Representative, 'Generalized System of Preferences' <https://ustr.gov/issue-areas/trade-development/preference-programs/generalized-system-preference-gsp> accessed 23 December 2015.

[82] Kuanpoth (n 77) 181-184.

[83] It is an annual report on the effectiveness of U.S. trade partners' protection of intellectual property rights. Office of the United States Trade Representative, 'USTR Releases Annual Special 301 Report on Intellectual Property Rights' <https://ustr.gov/about-us/policy-offices/press-office/press-releases/2015/april/ustr-releases-annual-special-301> accessed 23 December 2015.

[84] Muzaka (n 6) 156.

[85] H Knight, *Patent Strategy: For Researchers and Research Managers* (Chichester: John Wiley & Sons 1996) 91.

[86] Bureau of Industry Economics, *The Economics of Patents* (Canberra: Australian Government Publishing Service 1994) 8.

Pre-TRIPS, Indian firms were allowed to manufacture imitated patented pharmacological products for three years or less following their first production elsewhere.[87] However, post-TRIPS, Indian companies focused on selling generic drugs once the duration of the patent expired. This had a negative impact upon people suffering from fatal diseases.[88] This is despite the fact that it takes years for imitators to create a marketable imitation for the new products. Until then, innovators can still benefit financially, even without a patent.[89] In 2011, India resorted to its first compulsory license, in order to legally replicate a branded cancer drug and sell it at $160, when the original price of the patented medicine was $5050.[90] Issues arise when a developing country is permitted to reproduce a generic drug within the monopolistic period, and the low-price version could find a way back to industrial countries, undermining patent prices.[91] This may affect the effectiveness of the patent system to provide an incentive to reveal their innovative findings and to encourage further medical research. Some judicial decrees have also had an impact on the patent system's role. In *Kellogg v Wyeth*,[92] the court held that the manufacturer of branded medicine is liable for the harmful effects and injuries caused by generic versions. This is despite the fact that the branded medicine gained the approval of the Food and Drug Administration (FDA). These conflicting interests make it difficult to achieve a balance between generic industry permissions and patented medicines' rights. Additionally, the patent system can be unsatisfactory for the pharmaceutical companies themselves.

7. Patent System against Pharmaceutical Company

The patent system could not work well in the context of certain medicaments, because of the required characterises of the patent to be useful, novel and non-obvious and this could be incompatible with pharmaceutical industries on many grounds. Firstly, the drug efficacy cannot be verified at the time of application. Secondly, it is difficult to imagine that a drug would not be patented merely because scientific journals disclose trivial information about the drug, thereby affecting its novelty. Finally, the non-obviousness criterion entails that a drug should not be discovered

87 Horner (n 7) 391-392.

88 *Ibid* 399.

89 Bureau of Industry Economics (n 86) 8.

90 Horner (n 7) 399.

91 M Bloche & Elizabeth Jungman, 'Patent Immorality?' (2002) 2(3) The American Journal of Bioethics 48, 49.

92 Kellogg v Wyeth, (2010) 762 F Supp 2d 694 (District Court).

in the course of an ordinary expected procedure, which makes most successful drugs incapable of being patented.[93] The average gain, within a patented period, is $1.4 million annually per medicine, while the average cost of research for a new drug estimated between$300-800 million.[94] Additionally, patent law may provide limited protection to the patented-drugs because it allows other companies to invent around the invention.[95] Consequently, in 2011, the largest drug-maker in the world, Pfizer,[96] announced plans to reduce research and close a major study establishment in England, resulting in the loss of 9000 Jobs.[97] Investors are reluctant to enter the pharmaceutical business due to the current deficiencies in the patent law system. They see the current position of patent law as undeserving of risk.[98]

Moreover, patent procedures are regarded as time-consuming, as the period from the filing of a patent-application until the issuance of the decision is about three years.[99] Additionally, the US system does not accept a medicine before the FDA, through clinical trials, confirms that it is safe and efficient.[100] The whole procedure may last fourteen years.[101] The 20-year-exclusivity period starts from the time of filing an application.[102] This automatically reduces the period of monopoly.[103] The long proceedings required for the patentability of an item has an impact upon the community and the patentees. For instance, in 2011, this long process results in a lack of medicines, including life-saving medicines and anesthetics in surgery, in the US.[104] There are more than 650,000 pending patents due to a lack of experts available to examine the patentability of an item.[105] A shortage of medicines forced the FDA to adopt a more flexible approach and to 'loosen its grip' on the required approvals. This

---

93 Amanda Fachler, 'The Need for Reform in Pharmaceutical Protection: The Inapplicability of the Patent System to the Pharmaceutical Industry and the Recommendation of a Shift towards Regulatory Exclusivities' (2014) 24 Fordham Intellectual Property, Media & Entertainment Law J 1059, 1078-1085.

94 Dutta (n 48) 177.

95 Bureau of Industry Economics (n 86) 26.

96 One of the world's premier biopharmaceutical corporation.

97 Christopher Holman, 'Unpredictability in Patent Law and Its Effect on Pharmaceutical Innovation' (2011) 76 Missouri Law Review 645, 646.

98 *Ibid* 646.

99 Fachler (n 95) 1066.

100 *Ibid* 1065.

101 *Ibid*.

102 *Ibid* 1066.

103 *Ibid* 1067.

104 *Ibid* 1075.

105 Mattappally (n 19) 996.

flexibility in providing approvals necessary to manufacture drugs is to expedite the procedures for producing the needed drugs.[106] However, if the FDA, after investigating a medicine's efficiency, finds that a medicine is inefficient, it may compel the manufacturers to withdraw the medicine from the market and, in turn, the manufacturers suffer economic loss, and patients may suffer from the side effects of the medicine. Applying for patent protection for the same invention in different countries demands a particular way, an alternative *modus operandi*.[107] New drugs require experimental testing by patent examiners and this may result in confidential information becoming available to the public. This, in turn, could constitute grounds for patent invalidation on the basis of a medicine's prior use.[108] For the aforementioned reasons, there could be a persistent need to find an alternative to the patent system.

8. Other Means of Supporting New-Drugs beyond Patents

Because of the undesirable consequences of the patent system, there should be an alternative incentive for inventors. Such an alternative would be cheaper, avoiding the long monopolistic prices and minimising costs, and would be beneficial for both companies and the community. Research should be granted prizes for new drugs as an alternative incentive to develop and explore new drugs,[109] and the State should financially participate in reducing the research cost. Subsidising research by States may be through:[110] 1) investing over salary deduction for pensions and the profits would be for developing research; 2) encouraging donations for the research, such as from UK Cancer Research; 3) revenues of imposition tax on luxuries could be spend on research, or; 4) introducing a tax to fund governmental research.[111] However, these measures should not disproportionately affect citizens of low income. States should encourage national pharmaceutical manufacturing in cooperation with foreign investors; reducing tax on these factories; and permissions for real-estate purchase.[112]

[106] Fachler (n 95) 1075-1076.
[107] Morten Tvedt (n 56) 278-279.
[108] R S Crespi, *Patenting in the Biological Sciences*, (Chichester: John Wiley & Sons 1982) 78-79.
[109] Muzaka (n 6) 152 & 158.
[110] Bureau of Industry Economics (n 86) 41.
[111] Ragavan (n 28) 195.
[112] Mrazek et al (n 17) 337.

The aim of reducing the cost of patented drugs to ensure the price is limited to the cheapest possible cost of production and distribution could be through the creation of a Health Impact Fund (HIF).[113] This initiative would likely encourage research for new medicines by offering drug inventors, for an agreed period, remuneration and financial rewards corresponding to innovators' contributions to reducing human morbidity and improving universal healthcare.[114] In the patent registration country, there should be system controlling information of actual expenditure of patented medicines in order to specify the ratio of not higher-than-normal profitability.[115] Significantly, countries should encourage health insurance, at monthly low-cost payment, which will allow patients to purchase drugs that they cannot otherwise afford.[116] Health insurance would pay all these expenses from the revenue of those who remain healthy.

9. Conclusion

Indeed, the deficiencies described in this paper show that the system is flawed. Therefore, restructuring the patent system is unavoidable. Access to effective and affordable medicines is regarded as a prerequisite for global public health.[117] International trade regulations cannot compromise universal welfare.[118] The global community should take action to combat global health problems, rather than protecting only the intellectual property rights of pharmaceutical industries,[119] especially in cases which concern fatal and infectious diseases which require collaborated efforts and rapid implementation.[120] Fair balance between the rights of the pharmaceutical industries and the community is a necessity. Otherwise, rampant infectious diseases would prevail at dangerous levels, resulting in increased global mortality levels. Patent law could have positive effects. It could provide a motivation for research that can benefit wider society as the production of drugs enhances public health.[121] The

[113] Amitava Banerjee; Aidan Hollis & Thomas Pogge, 'The Health Impact Fund: Incentives for Improving Access to Medicines' (2010) 375(9709) The Lancet 166, 166-167.

[114] *Ibid*. See also Li (n 66) 23.

[115] Blum (n 17) 201.

[116] Andrew Jones, *The Elgar Companion to Health Economics* (Cheltenham: Edward Elgar 2012) 98.

[117] Muzaka (n 6) 152.

[118] Ragavan (n 28) 197-198.

[119] Muzaka (n 6) 151.

[120] *Ibid* 152.

[121] Ragavan (n 28) 35.

main rule is that one must receive remuneration equivalent to that which one has produced. Nevertheless, this does not automatically mean that the inventor is entitled to monopolise the knowledge for a disproportionately long time. Countries still need to reduce the cost of pioneering medical research through resorting to other motivational means. The result would be that the period of the monopoly of the product would decrease. This will enable follow up progress based on patented drugs.[122]

References

Action Programme on Essential Drugs 1979.

Agreement on Trade-related Aspects of Intellectual property Rights 1994 (TRIPS).

Amanda F., 'The Need for Reform in Pharmaceutical Protection: The Inapplicability of the Patent System to the Pharmaceutical Industry and the Recommendation of a Shift towards Regulatory Exclusivities' (2014) 24 *Fordham Intellectual Property, Media & Entertainment Law Journal* 1059-1098.

Avert, 'HIV And AIDS in South Africa' (2017) <https://www.avert.org/professionals/hiv-around-world/sub-saharan-africa/south-africa> accessed 20 April 2016.

Banerjee A., Hollis A. & Pogge T., 'The Health Impact Fund: Incentives for Improving Access to Medicines' (2010) 375(9709). *The Lancet* 166-169.

Bently L. & Sherman B., *Intellectual Property Law* (Oxford: Oxford University Press 2014).

Blum R., Herxheimer A., Stenzl C. & Woodcock J., *Pharmaceuticals and Health Policy* (New York: Holmes & Meier Publishers 1981).

Bloche M. & Jungman E., 'Patent Immorality?' (2002) 2(3). *The American Journal of Bioethics*, 48-49.

Chalmers J., *Legal Responses to HIV and AIDS* (Oxford: Hart Publishing 2008).

Crespi R., *Patenting in the Biological Sciences* (Chichester: John Wiley & Sons 1982).

Declaration on the Rights of Indigenous Peoples 2008 (DRIP).

Devlin A., 'Systemic Bias in Patent Law' (2012) 61 *DePaul Law Review* 57-111.

Dutta A., 'From Free Entry to Patent Protection: Welfare Implications for the Indian Pharmaceutical Industry' (2011) 93(1) *The Review of Economics and Statistics* 160-178.

[122] Devlin (n 15) 65.

Doha Declaration on the TRIPS Agreement and Public Health 2001 (Doha Declaration).

Farina L, 'Patent Law and the Sociology of Innovation' (2013) 2 *Wisconsin Law Review* 813-873.

General Council Decision 2003 on the Implementation of Paragraph 6 of the Doha Declaration on the TRIPS Agreement and Public Health.

Gibson J., *Patenting Lives: Life Patents, Culture and Development* (Cornwall: TJ international 2008).

Holman C., 'Unpredictability in Patent Law and Its Effect on Pharmaceutical Innovation' (2011) 76 *Missouri Law Review* 645-693.

Horner R., 'The Impact of Patents on Innovation, Technology Transfer and Health: A Pre- and Post-Trips Analysis of India's Pharmaceutical Industry' (2014) 19(3) *New Political Economy* 384-406.

International Covenant on Civil and Political Rights 1966.

International Covenant on Economic, Social and Cultural Rights 1966 (ICESCR).

Jones A., The Elgar Companion to Health Economics (Cheltenham: Edward Elgar 2012).

Kellogg v Wyeth, (2010) 762 F Supp 2d 694 (District Court).

Kirim A., 'Reconsidering Patents and Economic Development: A Case Study of the Turkish Pharmaceutical Industry' (1985) 13(2) *World Development* 219-236.

KSR International Co. v Teleflex Inc. (2007) 550 US 398 (US Supreme Court).

Knight H., Patent Strategy: For Researchers and Research Managers (Chichester: John Wiley & Sons 1996).

Kuanpoth J., Patent Rights in Pharmaceuticals in Developing Countries (Cheltenham: Edward Elgar 2010).

Li P., Health Technologies and International Intellectual Property (London: Routledge 2014).

Lisherness C., 'Patent Reissue Genus Claims: Harmful Evolution' (2003) 26 *Thomas Jefferson Law* Review 85- 101.

Mossialos E., Mrazek M. & Walley T., *Regulating Pharmaceuticals in Europe: Striving for Efficiency, Equity and Quality* (Berkshire: Open University Press 2004).

Mattappally J., 'Goliath Beats David: Undoing the Leahy-Smith America Invents Act's Harmful Effects on Small Businesses Comment' (2012) 58 *Loyola Law Review* 981-1034.

Mueller J., 'Taking TRIPS to India - Novartis, Patent Law, and Access to Medicines' (2007) 356(6) *The New England Journal of Medicine* 541-543.

Muzaka V., 'Prizes for Pharmaceuticals? Mitigating the Social ineffectiveness of the current

Pharma Letter, UAE's Julphar Inks Five-year Deal to Market Merck & Co Drugs (11 April 2014).

NHS, Schistosomiasis (bilharzia) <https://www.nhs.uk/conditions/schistosomiasis/> accessed 18 April 2018.

Office of the United States Trade Representative, 'Generalized System of Preferences' <https://ustr.gov/issue-areas/trade-development/preference-programs/generalized-system-preference-gsp> accessed 23 December 2015.

Office of the United States Trade Representative, 'Intellectual Property' <https://ustr.gov/issue-areas/intellectual-property> accessed 23 December 2015.

Office of the United States Trade Representative, 'USTR Releases Annual Special 301 Report on Intellectual Property Rights' <https://ustr.gov/about-us/policy-offices/press-office/press-releases/2015/april/ustr-releases-annual-special-301> accessed 23 December 2015.

Ragavan S., *Patent and Trade Disparities in Developing Countries* (Oxford: Oxford University Press 2012).

StopFakes, 'What is a Patent?' (7 July 2016) <http://www.stopfakes.gov/learn-about-ip/patents/about> accessed 12 December 2015.

Pharmaceutical Patent Arrangement' (2013) 34(1) *Third World Quarterly* 151-169.

Suh D., Manning W., Schondelmeyer S. & Hadsall R., 'Effect of Multiple-Source Entry on Price Competition after Patent Expiration in the Pharmaceutical Industry' (2000) 35(2) *Health Services Research* 529-547.

Tvedt M., 'One Worldwide Patent System: What's in it for Developing Countries?' (2010) 31(2) *Third World Quarterly* 277-293.

United States Code 2000.

Universal Declaration of Human Rights 1948 (UDHR).

World Health Organization, 'Saving Lives through the Promotion of Quality Medicines' <http://www.who.int/medicines/services/expertcommittees/pharmprep/qual_med_promo_save-lives/en/> accessed 13 December 2016.

World Health Organization, 'Schistosomiasis: WHO reports substantial treatment progress for school-age Children' (8 December 2017) <http://www.who.int/neglected_diseases/news/WHO_schistosomiasis_reports_substantial_treatment_progress_sac/en/> accessed 18 April 2018.

World Health Organization, 'Update 61 - WHO extends its SARS related travel advice to all of Taiwan province, China' (21 May 2003) <http://www.who.int/csr/don/2003_05_21a/en/> accessed 20 April 2016.

Yvette M., Germán V. & Enrique F., 'The Economics of Pharmaceuticals and Health Sector Reform in the Americas' (1998) 3(5) Revista Panamericana de Salud Pública 343-350. Bureau of Industry Economics,

The Economics of Patents (Canberra: Australian Government Publishing Service 1994).

Human Rights in a Hostile Environment: Can International Human Rights Law Effectively Constrain Immigration Detention in the United Kingdom?

Sarah Crowe[1]

SOAS

Summary. The United Kingdom's practice of immigration detention has been described as a 'dark stain' on its human rights record. A number of aspects of the UK's detention practice engage fundamental human rights, including the practice of indefinite and prolonged detention, the lesser procedural safeguards afforded to detainees and the detention of particularly vulnerable persons. This paper evaluates the utility of international human rights law as a tool of constraining these harmful detention practices. In exposing the limits of international human rights law in protecting the rights of immigration detainees, it is concluded that while claims of territorial sovereignty remain unchallenged and 'othering' of migrants continues, international human rights law will struggle to constrain—let alone abolish—immigration detention.

Introduction

The United Kingdom's practice of immigration detention has been described as a *'dark stain'* on its human rights record.[2] Immigration detention involves the deprivation of liberty for administrative purposes, viewed by the United Kingdom (UK) government to be '*...in the interests*

[1] Email: sarah.crowe121@gmail.com

[2] Liberty, *'Liberty's response to the draft Home Office DSO on Removal from Association and Temporary Confinement'* August 2016 at: https://www.liberty-human-rights.org.uk/sites/default/files/Liberty's%20Response%20to%20the%20DSO%20on%20Removal%20from%20Association%20and%20Temporary%20Confinement.pdf

of maintaining effective immigration control.'[3] The practice in the UK has come under increasing scrutiny in recent years. The UK maintains one of the largest detention estates in Europe,[4] with growing concerns raised at local and international levels that this practice is ineffective and damaging. In his 2016 review of the welfare of vulnerable persons in detention, commissioned by the UK Home Office, ex-prison ombudsman Stephen Shaw concluded that detention in the UK is used *'excessively, harmfully and ineffectively.'*[5]

Immigration detention involves an interference with a right that '*...the liberal legal order has staked much of its legitimacy upon defending*'[6] – the right to liberty. In addition, as will be seen, UK practice has called into question inferences with other internationally protected rights. However, sovereign rights are increasingly invoked over those of the non-citizen, leading to a '*creeping criminalisation*' of immigration.[7] This criminalisation of immigration is the cornerstone of the UK government's concerted efforts to create a 'hostile environment' for immigrants in the UK.[8] With the domestic political environment largely unable to constrain the UK's immigration detention practice, this paper seeks to assess the efficacy of international human rights law (IHRL) in offering an alternative means of protection to immigration detainees in the UK.

Section One provides an overview of UK immigration detention, outlining the political environment that has fuelled its growth, and the clash

---

[3] UK Home Office '*Section 55: Enforcement Instructions and Guidance*' para.55.1.1 at: https://assets.publishing.service.gov.uk/government/uploads/system/uploads/attachment_data/file/721605/Chapter-55-detention-v25..pdf (Hereinafter, 'EIG')

[4] Silverman, S and Hajela, R '*Briefing: Immigration Detention in the UK*' (2016) Migration Observatory, University of Oxford p.3 at: http://www.migrationobservatory.ox.ac.uk/sites/files/migobs/Immigration%20Detention%20Briefing.pdf (Hereinafter 'Silverman and Hajela')

[5] Shaw, S '*Review into the Welfare in Detention of Vulnerable Persons: A report to the Home Office by Stephen Shaw*' January 2016 p.22 at https://www.gov.uk/government/uploads/system/uploads/attachment_data/file/490782/52532_Shaw_Review_Accessible.pdf (Hereinafter, 'Shaw Review')

[6] Wilsher D '*Immigration Detention: Law, History, Politics*'(2012) Cambridge: Cambridge University Press p.xiii (Hereinafter, 'Wilsher')

[7] Flynn, M '*Who Must be Detained? Proportionality as a Tool for Critiquing Immigration Detention Policy*'(2012) Refugee Survey Quarterly, pp.1–29 p. 11

[8] Kirkup, J and Winnett, R '*Theresa May interview: 'We're going to give illegal migrants a really hostile reception*' (2012) Telegraph at: http://www.telegraph.co.uk/news/uknews/immigration/9291483/Theresa-May-interview-Were-going-to-give-illegal-migrants-a-really-hostile-reception.html

between sovereign power and universal human rights underlying this practice. The following sections examine concerning aspects of UK immigration detention practice through an IHRL framework. Section Two discusses the indefinite and often prolonged nature of detention in the UK, while Section Three turns to the lack of procedural safeguards available to immigration detainees. Section Four considers the detention of particularly vulnerable persons, contrary to government policy. The issue of the privatisation of detention raises concerns throughout this paper, as market forces for private security services impact the political dynamics of detention,[9] and profits are prioritised over detainee welfare.

The author advocates the abolition of immigration detention, viewing deprivation of liberty on the basis of immigration status as inherently discriminatory. It is nevertheless considered that detention is a present reality and therefore safeguards are required to assuage its harmful effects. As such, IHRL will be evaluated as a tool of constraining some of the UK's most harmful detention practices and its limits will be exposed.

Section One: An Overview of Immigration Detention in the UK

UK Immigration Detention Practice

Immigration detention in the UK has increased rapidly since the power to detain immigrants at administrative discretion was first introduced by the 1971 Immigration Act (IA). These powers have been subsequently amended by legislation over the ensuing decades, which has seen an increase in detention powers, combined with weakening of legal safeguards. When these powers were first introduced, it was not intended that they would facilitate routine or mass detention of asylum seekers and other immigrants.[10] Yet, as highlighted in a recent report by Amnesty International, the UK government has come to develop a '*…more relaxed approach to detention powers and the weakening of protection for detainees…*' an approach which '*…allows detention to be used as a matter of routine: because it is there – not because it is necessary…*'[11] Indeed, in

[9] Bacon, C '*The Evolution of Immigration Detention in the UK: the Involvement of Private Prison Companies*' (2005) RSC Working Paper no. 27 (Hereinafter, 'Bacon')

[10] Bacon p.5

[11] Amnesty International, '*A Matter of Routine: Immigration Detention in the UK*' (2017) p. 19, at: https://www.libertyhumanrights.org.uk/sites/default/files/A%20Matter%20Of%20Routine%20ADVANCE%20COPY.pdf

the year ending March 2018, 26,541 persons entered immigration detention and, on average, 2,758 individuals were detained at one time.[12]

The UK's detention estate consists of seven Immigration Removal Centres (IRCs), two Short-Term Holding Facilities, one pre-departure accommodation facility, and 30 holding rooms,[13] as well as a number of places in prisons.[14] The Home Office outsources the operation of the vast majority of detention facilities to private companies.[15] The companies who have typically been awarded these contracts include G4S Plc, Serco Plc, Mitie Group Plc, Geo Group and Tascor.[16] The UK runs one of the largest immigration detention estates in Europe,[17] with a capacity of approximately 3,200 places.[18]

Many detainees in the UK have claimed and been refused asylum, others have overstayed or have no visa, or are foreign national ex-offenders awaiting deportation. The Detained Fast Track (DFT) system detained asylum seekers whose cases were viewed as quickly resolvable.[19] It was suspended in 2015, however, following legal challenges over its lack of appropriate safeguards for vulnerable detainees.[20]

---

[12] UK Home Office '*National Statistics: How many people are detained or returned?*' May 2018, at: https://www.gov.uk/government/publications/immigration-statistics-year-ending-march-2018/how-many-people-are-detained-or-returned (Hereinafter, 'Detention Statistics')

[13] Griffiths, M and Silverman, S '*Immigration Detention in the UK*' (2019) Migration Observatory at: https://migrationobservatory.ox.ac.uk/resources/briefings/immigration-detention-in-the-uk/

[14] Bosworth, M '*Inside Immigration Detention*'(2014) Oxford: Oxford University Press p.3 (Hereinafter, 'Bosworth')

[15] Griffiths, M and Silverman, S '*Immigration Detention in the UK*' (2019) Migration Observatory at: https://migrationobservatory.ox.ac.uk/resources/briefings/immigration-detention-in-the-uk/

[16] *Ibid.*

[17] Global Detention Project, 'United Kingdom Immigration Detention' (2016) at: https://www.globaldetentionproject.org/countries/europe/united-kingdom

[18] Griffiths, M and Silverman, S '*Immigration Detention in the UK*' (2019) Migration Observatory at: https://migrationobservatory.ox.ac.uk/resources/briefings/immigration-detention-in-the-uk/

[19] UK Home Office '*Detained Fast Track Processes*' p.4 at: https://www.gov.uk/government/uploads/system/uploads/attachment_data/file/370322/Detained_Fast_Track_Processes_v6_0.pdf

[20] UK Home Office '*Written Statement made by: The Minister of State for Immigration (James Brokenshire)*' July 2015 at: http://www.parliament.uk/documents/commons-vote-office/July%202015/2%20July/6-Home-Asylum.pdf

Under UK domestic law, immigration detention is only permitted where there is statutory power to detain, as contained in the IA 1971[21] and extended by several other immigration statutes. The detention centres are regulated by the Detention Centre Rules (DCR) 2001 and in Section 55 of the Enforcement Instruction and Guidance (EIG) which indicates, *inter alia*, who is suitable to be detained. The EIG asserts that detention is usually appropriate:

> To effect removal;
> To establish a person's identity or basis of claim; or
> Where there is reason to believe that the person will fail to comply with conditions upon release.[22]

Limitations on the Power to Detain

At common law, four principles articulated in *R (Hardial Singh) v Governor of Durham Prison* require that detention must only be: (1) for the purpose of deportation; (2) for a reasonable period; (3) used where is reasonable prospect of removal; and (4) that removal proceedings must be pursued with due diligence.[23] These principles have been endorsed by the UK Supreme Court.[24]

European Union (EU) law will not be examined in this paper, however, at present, it does place some limitations on the UK's power to detain. Free movement principles dictate that EU citizens may only be detained in extremely exceptional circumstances.[25] The Reception Conditions Directive 2003/9/EC established minimum standards for the reception of asylum-seekers, however its lack of precision has accommodated detention practices, including the DFT.[26] The Asylum Procedures Directive 2005/85/EC prohibits detention for the sole reason that an individual seeks asylum.[27] The UK has opted out of the majority of subsequent Directives which provide more specific limitations on immigration detention, including the Returns Directive 2008/115/EC which imposed a time limit of six months, extendable to 18 months, amongst other

[21] Sch.2(16) IA, Sch.2(21) IA, Sch.3(2)(1) IA
[22] EIG para.55.1.1
[23] [1983] EWHC 1 (QB)
[24] *Walumba Lumba & Kadian Mighty v SSHD* [2011] UKSC 12
[25] Case C215/03 *Oulane v Minister voor Vreemdelingenzaken en Integratie* [2005] ECR I 1215
[26] Wilsher, p.187
[27] Art.18

safeguards.[28] Consequently, EU law places only limited restrictions on the UK's power to detain.

Limitations placed upon immigration detention by IHRL will be discussed throughout, and so only a brief outline is given here. Immigration detention interferes with one of the most fundamental rights in any democratic society, the right to liberty.[29] This is contained in several IHRL instruments. Of particular relevance are Article 5(1)(f) European Convention on Human Rights (ECHR)[30] and Article 9(1) International Covenant on Civil and Political Rights (ICCPR).[31] In addition, detention may engage other rights, including, but not limited to, the right to be free from torture, inhuman and degrading treatment,[32] the right of detainees to be treated humanely,[33] the right to life[34] and respect for private and family life.[35] Furthermore, international refugee law prohibits the imposition of penalties on refugees for unauthorised entry as well as unnecessary restrictions on refugees' freedom of movement.[36]

There is a plethora of 'soft law' measures containing minimum standards for detention, including the UN Body of Principles for the Protection of All Persons under Any Form of Detention or Imprisonment (BOP)[37] the UN High Commissioner for Refugees (UNHCR) Detention Guidelines,[38] the UNHCR Executive Committee Conclusion (ECC) no.

---

28 This lengthy time limit has been heavily criticised: Baldaccini, A '*The European Directive on Returns: Principles and Protests*'(2010) 28(4) Refugee Survey Quarterly 114-38 p.130

29 Wilsher p.xiii

30 Convention for the Protection of Human Rights and Fundamental Freedoms (as amended) 1950 ETS 5 (ECHR), incorporated into UK law by the Human Rights Act 1998.

31 999 UNTS 171 (ICCPR)

32 *inter alia,* Art.3 ECHR; Art.7 ICCPR; UN Convention against Torture and Other Cruel, Inhuman or Degrading Treatment or Punishment (UNCAT) 1984, 1465 UNTS 85

33 Art.10 ICCPR; Art.11 UNCAT

34 *inter alia,* Art.2 ECHR, Art.6 ICCPR

35 *inter alia,* Art.8 ECHR, Art.17 ICCPR

36 Art.31(1)-(2), Art.26 Convention Relating to the Status of Refugees 1951 189 UNTS 150

37 UNGA, 9 December 1988, A/RES/43/173

38 UNHCR '*Guidelines on the Applicable Criteria and Standards Relating to the Detention of Asylum-seekers and Alternatives to Detention*'(2012) at: http://www.unhcr.org/505b10ee9.pdf

44[39] and UN General Assembly (UNGA)/Human Rights Council resolutions calling for an end to arbitrary immigration detention.[40]

A Hostile Environment

The proliferation of immigration detention in the UK – and across Europe and beyond - must be understood in a context of growing political hostility towards migrants. Anti-immigration rhetoric, propagated by certain politicians and media outlets, constructs migrants as threats to British security, people and values.[41] The alien 'other' is depicted as 'criminal,' 'bogus' and 'risky'[42] and is vilified in order to deepen divisions between 'us' and 'them.' This relies on racialised and gendered constructions of difference; the (masculine) rational, developed, humane, superior versus the (feminine) aberrant, undeveloped and inferior.[43] This is perpetuated through dehumanising language, such as descriptions of 'floods' or 'swarms' of migrants[44] and reliance upon dichotomies including deserving/undeserving, authorised/unauthorised, desirable/undesirable and civilised/uncivilised.

Bhui argues that the practice of immigration detention is a manifestation of historical, colonial processes that have encouraged racism and criminalisation of people of colour to entrench their marginalisation.[45] Through the lens of race, immigration detention can be seen as a mechanism of consolidating state authority – one that reinforces structural power and race relations. This is achieved through the control and subjugation of those considered undesirable or 'other.' As Bosworth and

[39] (1968) no.44 (XXXVII)

[40] UNGA Res.63/184 '*Protection of Migrants,*'(2009) 63rd sess, [9]A/RES/63/184; UNGA Res 64/166 '*Protection of Migrants*'(2010) 64th sess A/RES/64/166 [4(a)]; UNGA, Human Rights Council, Resolution 15/16'*Human Rights of* Migrants'(2010)A/HRC/RES/15/16

[41] Malloch, M and Stanley, E '*The Detention of Asylum-Seekers in the UK: Representing Risk, Managing the Dangerous*'(2005) Punishment & Society 1462-4745; Vol 7(1): 53–71 p.55

[42] Welch, M and Schuster, L '*Detention of asylum seekers in the UK and USA: Deciphering noisy and quiet constructions*'(2005) Punishment & Society 1462-4745; Vol 7(4): 397–417

[43] Said, E '*Orientalism*'(1985) London:Peregrine p.300

[44] for example, Elgot, J and Taylor, M '*Calais crisis: Cameron condemned for 'dehumanising' description of migrants*' (2015) Guardian available at: https://www.theguardian.com/uk-news/2015/jul/30/david-cameron-migrant-swarm-language-condemned

[45] Bhui, H S, '*The place of 'race' in understanding immigration control and the detention of foreign nationals*'(2016) Criminology & Criminal Justice 2016, Vol.16(3) 267-285

Kellezi argue, detention centres in the UK feed into and perpetuate a conception of British identity based on exclusion and racialisation.[46] That immigration detention centres are disproportionately populated with people of colour is no coincidence. As Bosworth, Parmar, and Vázquez highlight:

> 'Though rarely explicitly acknowledged, concerns about race and ethnicity animate many of the state and popular responses to the growing number of migrants and refugees seeking entry. Racial profiling, fears about national security and processes of 'othering' convene within concerns about mobility.'[47]

For immigration detainees who are white, mainly Eastern European migrants, Bhui observes that while such persons usually conform to racialised understandings of what it means to be European, xenophobic hostility towards Eastern Europeans subjects them to a framing as 'other' that enables the authorities to detain them. This process of distancing and dehumanising is crucial to the operation of the immigration detention system.

While Bhui rightly connects modern immigration enforcement practice to enduring historic colonial and racist attitudes, this process of 'othering' has intensified in recent decades as anti-immigrant sentiment has permeated popular discourse. Such sentiment was pervasive during the 2016 referendum campaign that led 59.1% of the British public to vote in favour of the UK leaving the EU. Public discourse surrounding the campaign to leave the EU focused on the protection of British sovereignty through promises to 'take back' sovereignty and secure borders. This narrative was exemplified by the widely condemned poster promoted by leading Brexit campaigner Nigel Farage, depicting a queue of migrants/refugees with the caption *'Breaking Point: the EU has failed us all…we must break free of the EU and take back control of our borders.'*[48]

---

[46] Bosworth, M and Kellezi, B, '*Citizenship and Belonging in a Women's Immigration Detention Centre*' (2013) p.2 In C. Philips and C. Webster (Eds.). (2014). New Directions in Race and Ethnicity. Abingdon: Routledge; Criminal Justice, Borders and Citizenship Research Paper No. 2448450

[47] Bosworth, M, Parmar, A and Vázquez, Y *'Race, Criminal Justice, and Migration Control: Enforcing the Boundaries of Belonging'* (2018) p.1 Oxford University Press

[48] Wright, O *'EU referendum: Nigel Farage's anti-migrant poster like 1930s fascist propaganda, says George Osborne'* (2016) Independent at: https://www.independent.co.uk/news/uk/politics/eu-referendum-poster-nigel-farage-polls-michael-gove-a7089946.html

Disillusionment with the EU, disenfranchisement of large sections of society and rising nationalism are inextricably linked to xenophobia and feelings of loss of control/sovereignty. In the UK, austerity measures and the resulting entrenchment of poverty and hardship have resulted in further feelings of powerlessness and disenfranchisement in many communities, with immigrants becoming a convenient scapegoat invoked by certain media outlets and politicians to explain away the country's economic woes.[49] This has resulted in increased popularity of far-right parties across Europe in recent years, who have typically blamed immigrants for society's problems. It is within this environment that '*...detention has come to take on important symbolic functions by demonstrating control of borders for citizens and potential future arrivals alike.*'[50]

Increasingly restrictive immigration policies have further criminalised undocumented immigrants. Such policies are part of a concerted effort by the UK Government to create a '*...hostile environment for illegal migration.*'[51] While it is believed the concept of the 'hostile environment' had been advocated by former Labour Home Secretary, Alan Johnson, in 2009-2010, it was introduced as official government policy in 2012 by then-Home Secretary, Theresa May (later promoted to Prime Minister). The intended impact of that policy was to make life for unauthorised immigrants living in the UK as difficult as possible.[52] In addition to increasingly restrictive immigration laws, the hostile environment policy sees the role of immigration enforcement delegated to members of the public – to landlords, bank managers and NHS doctors and nurses. In March 2019, the High Court declared the '*right to rent*' policy, requiring

---

[49] Redress, '*Austerity & Legal Aid: Impact on the vulnerable*' (2014) [143] at: http://www.redress.org/downloads/publications/10Oct2014-austerity-and-legal-aid-conference-paper.pdf

[50] Sampson, R and Mitchell, G '*Global Trends in Immigration Detention and Alternatives to Detention Practical, Political and Symbolic Rationales*'(2013)*JMHS Vol.(1)3 97-121 p.107*

[51] Kirkup, J and Winnett, R '*Theresa May interview: 'We're going to give illegal migrants a really hostile reception*' Telegraph, 25 May 2012, at: http://www.telegraph.co.uk/news/uknews/immigration/9291483/Theresa-May-interview-Were-going-to-give-illegal-migrants-a-really-hostile-reception.html

[52] Independent Chief Inspector of Borders and Immigration '*An inspection of the 'hostile environment' measures relating to driving licences and bank accounts*' (2016) p.12 https://assets.publishing.service.gov.uk/government/uploads/system/uploads/attachment_data/file/567652/ICIBI-hostile-environment-driving-licences-and-bank-accounts-January-to-July-2016.pdf

landlords to check the immigration status of prospective tenants, as incompatible with the ECHR owing to its racially discriminatory impact.[53]

The hostile environment policy continued to permeate the approach of the Home Office of Theresa May's government during her tenure as prime minister from 2016 to 2019. As highlighted in 2018 by the UN Special Rapporteur on contemporary forms of racism, racial discrimination, xenophobia and related intolerance,[54]the implementation of this policy has had a disastrous impact on the rights of immigrants and black and ethnic minority communities in the UK, has deepened divisions, hampered integration, and promoted racism and scapegoating.

The continued detrimental impact of the hostile environment policy was recently exposed by the Windrush scandal. The scandal erupted when it emerged that the children of the Windrush Generation[55] were being wrongly told by the UK Home Office that they had no right to be in the UK, purportedly as they did not have the correct documents, despite being British citizens and living and working in the UK their whole lives. As a result, they were being detained and/or deported, or threatened with such measures. Yet, the deeply problematic treatment of the Windrush generation is not an unfortunate administrative oversight by the Home Office. Rather, it is a direct result of the deliberate hostile environment policy that has infiltrated the department's policies and working since 2012. As Satbir Singh, Chief Executive of JCWI stated:

> 'The treatment of the Windrush generation is no accident. It is precisely what happens when an anti-immigrant dogma takes over at the Home Office. Despite warnings, Theresa May chose to create a system that was designed to be as hostile as possible, whatever the cost.'[56]

While the Windrush scandal rightly sparked national outrage, the hostile environment policy remains intact – despite a government re-brand to

---

[53] *R (Joint Council for the Welfare of Immigrants) v Secretary of State for the Home Department* [2019] EWHC 452 (Admin)

[54] Dearden, L '*UN tells UK government to stop forcing NHS and landlords to enforce 'hostile environment'*' (2018) Independent at: https://www.independent.co.uk/news/uk/home-news/un-uk-nhs-landlords-immigration-hostile-environment-special-rapporteur-brexit-a8347481.html

[55] The Windrush generation are those people and their descendants who arrived to live in the UK from the Caribbean between 1948 and 1971, upon the invitation of the UK government owing to post-war labour shortages.

[56] JCWI '*Dossier of Failure - Windrush and the Hostile Environment*' (2018) at: https://www.jcwi.org.uk/news-and-policy/dossier-of-failure-windrush-and-hostile-environment

'compliant environment'[57] - and thousands of its victims, those less able to appeal to public sympathies, go largely unnoticed, languishing in detention centres across the UK.

Territorial Sovereignty vs. Universal Human Rights

Sovereignty in the above context means territorial sovereignty, or the *'...territorialisation of political rule by means of state formation.'*[58] This entails the exercise of political authority within a clearly delimited territory and a monopoly over the legitimate use of violence.[59] A cornerstone of sovereignty is the principle that states enjoy the right to distinguish internal from external, which is, in large part, achieved through border control. The sovereign authority uses the juridical/political system to distinguish the politically qualified (political life) from the politically non-qualified (bare life or *homo sacer),* placing the latter into a state of exception.[60] This divides the internal from external; political life from bare life; citizen from alien.

Traditionally, international law has entrenched sovereignty through the principle of non-intervention in states' domestic affairs.[61] Feminist perspectives highlight that this is reinforced through international law's structural bias, which maintains a public/private dichotomy, privileging the public sphere and reinforcing the patriarchal concentration of power in the elite state, legitimising notions of sovereign equality, territorial integrity and the use of force to defend those attributes.[62]

Cornelisse argues that immigration detention is state-sanctioned violence used to defend and reproduce territorial sovereignty.[63] The detention of persons without criminal charge or trial due to their immigration

---

[57] Farrer, M, Grierson, J and Sparrow, A *'Sajid Javid disowns 'hostile environment' phrase in first outing as home secretary'* (2018) Guardian at: https://www.theguardian.com/politics/live/2018/apr/30/theresa-may-new-home-secretary-amber-rudd-quits-politics-live

[58] Grimm, D *'Sovereignty: The Origin and Future of a Political and Legal Concept'*(2015) Columbia University Press (Hereinafter, 'Grimm') p.77

[59] Marong, C *'Protecting the Public? Challenging the Indefinite Preventative Detention of Non-Citizens'* (2014) UCL Journal of Law and Jurisprudence Vol.3(1) 115-143 p.137

[60] Agamben, G *'Homo Sacer: Sovereign Power and Bare Life'*(1998) Stanford University Press; Agamben, G *'State of Exception'*(2005) University of Chicago Press

[61] Grimm, p.80

[62] Charlesworth, H, Chinkin, C, Wright, S *'Feminist Approaches to International Law'*(1991) American Journal of International Law, Vol. 85(4) 613-645 p.622

[63] Cornelisse, p.231

status is justified through the understanding that states have the sovereign prerogative to control borders. Thus, the right to detain unauthorised aliens '*...remains a closely guarded touchstone of statehood.*'[64]

The concept of sovereignty-as-non-interference has been gradually eroding since the end of World War II, following the creation of the UN in 1945 and emergence of IHRL, as well as the establishment of the EU. The UN Universal Declaration of Human Rights 1948[65] and subsequent IHRL treaties are predicated on the aspiration of the universality of human rights, that:

> 'Human rights are rights held simply by virtue of being a human person. They are part and parcel of the integrity and dignity of the human being. They are thus rights that cannot be given or withdrawn at will by any domestic legal system.'[66]

While the concept of universality of human rights is by no means uncontested,[67] IHRL places obligations on state parties to respect the rights contained therein. States are, at least theoretically, no longer immune to external interference.

When rights interferences are justified by territorial sovereignty, however, IHRL does not always provide adequate protection. In its desire to maintain domestic political legitimacy and a '*hostile environment,*' the UK government deprives migrants of their liberty and other rights, viewing them as non-citizens, unauthorised and illegitimate. This suggests that certain categories of persons are less entitled to human rights, challenging the universality of human rights.[68] The tension between the sovereign right to control borders and the principles of equality, non-discrimination and universality that underpin human rights lies at the heart of immigration detention.

---

[64] Bryan, I Langford, P '*The Lawful Detention of Unauthorised Aliens under the European System for the Protection of Human Rights*'(2011) Nordic Journal of International Law 80 193–218 p.194 (Hereinafter, 'Bryan & Langford')

[65] UNGA Res 217 A(III)

[66] Higgins, R '*Problems and Process: International Law and How We Use It*' (1995) Oxford University Press p.95

[67] e.g Mutua, M, '*Human Rights:A Political and Cultural Critique*'(2002) Philadelphia:University of Pennsylvania Press p.46

[68] Wilsher, p.124

Section Two: The Power to Detain Indefinitely

The UK is an '*outlier...both within the EU and further afield*' in having no time limit on the duration of immigration detention.[69] Many are detained prolonged periods, not knowing whether they will be released back into the community or removed from the UK. Unlike convicted prisoners who count down the days until their release date, immigration detainees are left '*in limbo*', counting the days up.[70] This section examines the role of IHRL in constraining – or, rather, legitimising – this controversial practice.

Prolonged and Indefinite Immigration Detention

Home Office policy requires immigration detention to be '*...used sparingly, and for the shortest period necessary.*'[71] This includes a presumption in favour of release and commitment to using alternatives to detention.[72]

There is no maximum time limit for immigration detention in the UK. This means that detainees are held indefinitely in detention, with no idea if and when they will be released. This lack of time limit has allowed for detainees to be held for unacceptably long periods of time. As was highlighted by HM Inspectorate of Prisons in its report on Harmondsworth IRC, the continuing lack of time limit had led to detention for '*excessively long periods*' and that '*23 men had been detained for over a year and one man had been held for over 4.5 years.*'[73] Across the detention estate in 2017, 80% (22,593 people) of detainees were detained for less than two months, 16% (4,491 people) were detained for between two and six months and three percent (935 people) were detained for between six and 12 months.[74] Of the less than one percent remaining, 225 people had been detained for over a year, 194 people had been detained for between

---

[69] All Party Parliamentary Group on Refugees & All Party Parliamentary Group on Migration 'T*he Report of the Inquiry into the Use of Immigration Detention in the United Kingdom*'(2015) p.24 (Hereinafter, 'APPG *Inquiry*')

[70] *Ibid.*p.19

[71] EIG para.55.1.3

[72] *Ibid.* para.55.20

[73] HMIP '*Harmondsworth immigration removal centre – persistent failings in safety and respect*' (2018) at: https://www.justiceinspectorates.gov.uk/hmiprisons/media/press-releases/2018/03/harmondsworth-immigration-removal-centre-persistent-failings-in-safety-and-respect/

[74] Association of Visitors to Immigration Detainees, '*Immigration Detention Statistics for 2017*' (2018) http://www.aviddetention.org.uk/news-events/news/immigration-detention-statistics-2017

one and two years, 27 people had been detained for between two and three years, and three people had been detained for three to four years. One person was released, having been detained for five years (at least 1,845 days).[75]

The UK courts have found prolonged detention to comply with the *Hardial Singh* principles, for example detention periods of 40[76] and 53 months.[77] What constitutes a 'reasonable period' may depend on *inter alia*, risks of re-offending, the merit of appeals pursued by the detainee or the possibility of return.[78] Furthermore, the Supreme Court has reiterated that there is no legal requirement for a time limit.[79]

As noted, the UK opted out of the EU Returns Directive, which imposes a maximum time limit. The only other EU Member State to do so, Ireland, has in place a 21-day time limit.[80] In comparison to other European countries, the UK stands alone in refusing to adopt a legal time limit. In France, for example, the limit is 90 days.[81]In Germany's tiered system, there is a six week limit on custody to secure departure, extendable to six months if an immigration detainee hinders their deportation, while asylum seekers may generally be detained in transit for up to 19 days.[82] In Hungary, the court may extend detention for 60 day periods, up to a maximum limit of six months detention in total.[83]

Common reasons for prolonged detention include difficulties in obtaining travel documents, non-cooperation of detainees,[84] perceived likelihood of absconding or re-offending and '*bureaucratic inertia.*'[85] There appears to be a *de facto* presumption against release for ex-offenders, and

[75] *Ibid.*

[76] *R(Davies) v Secretary of State for the Home Department* (SSHD) [2010] EWHC 2656 (Admin)

[77] *R(Giwa) v SSHD* [2013] EWHC 3189 (Admin)

[78] *Walumba Lumba*

[79] *R(on the application of Nouazli) v SSHD* [2016] UKSC 16 [67]

[80] Gower, M *'Immigration Detention in the UK: An Overview'*(2015) House of Commons Briefing Paper Number 7294 p.16 at: http://researchbriefings.files.parliament.uk/documents/CBP-7294/CBP-7294.pdf

[81] Global Detention Project *'Immigration Detention in France'* (2019) at: https://www.globaldetentionproject.org/countries/europe/france

[82] Global Detention Project *'Immigration Detention in Germany'* (2019) at: https://www.globaldetentionproject.org/countries/europe/germany

[83] Global Detention Project *'Immigration Detention in Hungary'* (2019) at: https://www.globaldetentionproject.org/countries/europe/hungary

[84] HM Inspectorate of Prisons (HMIP) and Independent Chief Inspector of Borders and Immigration, '*The effectiveness and impact of immigration detention casework*' (2012) p.8 at: http://icinspector.independent.gov.uk/wp-content/uploads/2012/12/Immigration-detention-casework-2012-FINAL.pdf

[85] *R(BA) v SSHD [2011] EWHC 2748 (Admin)*[237]

detention can be prolonged by lack of judicial oversight or legal representation.[86] Furthermore, it should not be overlooked that the detention estate is run by a *'large, politically and economically powerful private industry'* that has a vested interest in, and increasing influence over, the policy to maintain prolonged/indefinite detention.[87]

Inefficacy and Cost of Detention

Despite the UK government's insistence that detention is '*...in the interests of maintaining effective immigration control'*,[88] in the year ending March 2018, less than half (46%) of detainees leaving detention were removed from the UK. This indicates that detention is an ineffective means of removal, which is its stated purpose.[89] Furthermore, evidence demonstrating that the longer an individual is detained, the less likely they are to be removed from the UK,[90] demonstrates that prolonged detention is futile.

Indefinite detention has a devastating human cost. Uncertainty over the duration of detention is one of its most distinctive and unpleasant features. This often provokes feelings of hopelessness and fear, as one detainee describes:

> 'You know, you can't live a life, not knowing what's gonna happen tomorrow...The door is locked. You don't know what's gonna happen tomorrow.'[91]

Bosworth has found consistent evidence that detention has a negative impact on mental health, which increases the longer detention persists.[92] Research demonstrates that prolonged detention weakens formerly healthy persons[93] and deterioration in mental health can be directly correlated to detention beyond one month.[94] This will be discussed further in Section Four.

[86] See Section Three

[87] Bacon, p.25

[88] EIG para.55.1.1

[89] *Detention Statistics*

[90] APPG *Inquiry*, p.22

[91] Bosworth, p.162

[92] Shaw Review, p.305

[93] Jesuit Refugee Service*'Becoming Vulnerable in Detention'* (2010) p.71 at: http://www.europarl.europa.eu/document/activities/cont/201110/20111014ATT29338/20111014ATT29338EN.pdf (Hereinafter 'JRS')

[94] APPG *Inquiry*, p.19

In addition to this startling human cost, the financial cost of detention for the taxpayer is also very high. Between April 2013 and March 2017, the UK government spent £523.5 million on running the immigration detention estate, plus approximately £16.2 million paid in compensation for unlawful detention.[95] This constitutes an enormous amount of taxpayers' money being poured into a system that has both a devastating human cost and does not even achieve its stated objectives.

Detention, particularly prolonged/indefinite detention, is ineffective and disproportionate in terms of human and financial cost, condemned by the UNHCR as '*...inconsistent with the UK's rich human rights heritage.'*[96] The need for a time limit has been emphasised by UN bodies including the Committee Against Torture (CAT)[97] and the HRC,[98] as well as UK independent inspectorates[99] and human rights groups.[100]

The government has consistently rejected the idea of introducing a time limit for detention. During the passage of the IA 2016, an amendment to introduce a time limit was rejected. The government has maintained this position notwithstanding pressure from the abovementioned groups. In July 2016, the Home Affairs Select Committee raised con-

---

95 Bulman, M '*More than £500m spent on UK immigration detention over four years' (*2018) Independent at: https://www.independent.co.uk/news/uk/home-news/uk-immigration-detention-centre-cost-taxpayer-brexit-eu-migrants-a8195251.html

96 UNHCR '*Inquiry into the use of Immigration Detention: Written Evidence to the Parliamentary Joint* Committee'(2014)pp.5-6 at: http://www.refworld.org/docid/54f590ab4.html

97 CAT '*Concluding observations on the sixth periodic report of the United Kingdom of Great Britain and Northern Ireland*'(2019) CAT/C/GBR/CO/6 [54] (Hereinafter, 'CAT 2019')

98 HRC '*Concluding observations on the seventh periodic report of the United Kingdom of Great Britain and Northern Ireland*' (2015) CCPR/C/GBR/CO/7 [21] (Hereinafter, 'HRC Conc.obs')

99 e.g HMIP *'Report on an unannounced inspection of Yarl's Wood Immigration Removal Centre'* 2015 p.21 at: https://www.justiceinspectorates.gov.uk/hmiprisons/wp-content/uploads/sites/4/2015/08/Yarls-Wood-web-2015.pdf (Hereinafter 'HMIP YW') HMIP *'Report on an unannounced inspection of Colnbrook Immigration Removal Centre'* 2016 p.28 at https://www.justiceinspectorates.gov.uk/hmiprisons/wp-content/uploads/sites/4/2016/07/Colnbrook-Web-2016.pdf ; HMIP HMIP *'Report on an unannounced inspection of Harmondsworth Immigration Removal Centre'* 2018 at: https://www.justiceinspectorates.gov.uk/hmiprisons/inspections/heathrow-immigration-removal-centre-harmondsworth-site-2/

100 e.g Liberty, '*The case for a time limit on immigration detention has never been clearer*' (2016) at https://www.liberty-human-rights.org.uk/news/blog/case-time-limit-immigration-detention-has-never-been-clearer

cerns about the length of time individuals were being detained, arguing that '*further legal interventions, such as a statutory time limit on detention, will need to be considered if there has not been a significant impact on the length of detention.*'[101]

More recently, however, there have been indications that the government may be beginning to soften its stance on introducing a time limit. The most recent Shaw review, commissioned by the UK government as a follow up to the 2016 review and published in July 2018, was highly critical of continuing detention practices, particularly in relation to the detention of vulnerable individuals. The report found that while the number of those detained each year since the last review has decreased since the initial Shaw Review, the number of those detained for long periods, over six months, has actually increased, described as '*deeply troubling.*'[102] The publishing of this follow-up review has exerted further pressure on the government to review its detention practices, including to introduce a time limit. In the follow up review, however, Shaw observed that '*…at present, the case for a time limit has been articulated more as a slogan than as a fully developed policy proposal.*' [103]

Alternatives to Detention

Despite the presumption in favour of release, less intrusive alternatives are not routinely considered.[104] The International Detention Coalition argues that alternatives can '*prevent unnecessary detention and...resolve cases in a fair, timely and humane manner from a community setting.*'[105]

[101] Home Affairs Select Committee Q4 2015, HC 22 at https://publications.parliament.uk/pa/cm201617/cmselect/cmhaff/22/22.pdf

[102] Shaw, S, '*Assessment of government progress in implementing the report on the welfare in detention of vulnerable persons: A follow-up report to the Home Office by Stephen Shaw*' (2018) p.viii available at: https://assets.publishing.service.gov.uk/government/uploads/system/uploads/attachment_data/file/728376/Shaw_report_2018_Final_web_accessible.pdf (Hereinafter 'Follow-up Shaw Review')

[103] *Ibid.*

[104] Shaw Review, p.22.

[105] International Detention Coalition '*There Are Alternatives: A handbook for preventing unnecessary immigration detention (revised edition)*'(2015) p.II at:http://idcoalition.org/publication/there-are-alternatives-revised-edition/ (Hereinafter 'IDC')

Alternatives should observe the principle of minimum intervention,[106] and may include:

> '...registration and/or deposit of documents, bond/bail, reporting conditions, community release and supervision, designated residence, electronic monitoring or home curfew.'[107]

The UK uses some of these measures,[108] but does not do so widely or consistently.[109] Effective alternatives require a pragmatic shift towards case resolution based upon respect and empowerment of migrants as rights holders.[110] This involves constructive engagement with individuals throughout, without coercive enforcement measures,[111] clearly informing individuals of their rights and responsibilities, providing material support and legal aid, and tailored case management.[112]

There is a need for further research into and evaluation of alternatives to detention. Research does suggest, however, that alternatives to detention are capable of producing high compliance rates,[113] in addition to the substantial saving in human and financial cost, suggesting such alternatives are potentially more effective than detention. In the follow-up Shaw review, Professor Mary Bosworth conducts a review on alternatives to detention, and, while noting the gaps in academic research an evaluations of alternatives used internationally, Professor Bosworth nevertheless concludes that:

> '...well-funded, and well-supported case-management programs offering legal advice, housing and access to social and health care have high levels of compliance with all stages of the immigration system, including removal.'[114]

In his initial review, Shaw warned that such an approach would require a '*cultural shift*' due to the current excessive use of detention.[115] In his fol-

---

106 UNHCR and OHCHR Global Roundtable on Alternatives to Detention of Asylum-Seekers, Refugees, Migrants and Stateless Persons Geneva, 11-12 (2011) at:http://www.unhcr.org/536a00576.pdf (Hereinafter 'Global Roundtable')

107 *Ibid.* paras 20-21

108 See Section Three

109 APPG *Inquiry*, p.25

110 IDC, p.II

111 *Ibid.*

112 APPG *Inquiry*, p.26

113 Global Roundtable, p.4

114 Follow-up Shaw Review, pp.119-120

115 Shaw Review, p.22

low-up report, Shaw recommends a well-funded case management system, which he views to be particularly important in managing vulnerability.[116] Shaw observes that the Home Office has made little effort to explore such approaches since his initial review. Shaw also highlights in his follow-up review that the progression of such approaches is likely to be hampered by current Home Office policy and legislation restricting access to services and participation in society for those with uncertain immigration status.[117]

International Human Rights Law

While the UK political landscape has allowed indefinite immigration detention to continue, can the international human rights system provide an alternative mechanism to constrain this harmful practice? Immigration detention engages the right to liberty and security of person, a fundamental, although not absolute, right protected by IHRL. This right contains a prohibition of arbitrary deprivations of liberty. Deprivation of liberty entails objective and subjective elements: 1) confinement to a particular restricted space for a '*not negligible length of time*' and 2) lack of valid consent.[118] Differing interpretations of 'arbitrariness' have produced conflicting views over the legitimacy of indefinite and prolonged immigration detention.

European Court of Human Rights

The ECtHR considers the right to liberty as fundamental in any democratic society.[119] Art.5 ECHR guarantees the right to liberty and security of person, and specifically permits immigration detention under Art.5(1)(f) in two circumstances: 1) to prevent unauthorised entry or 2) for the purposes of deportation/extradition. Detention must also be '*in accordance with a procedure prescribed by law.*' This legality principle extends beyond mere compliance with substantive and procedural rules of national law,[120] and requires that detention should not be arbitrary,[121] corresponding with the purpose of Art.5.[122]

---

[116] Follow-up Shaw Review, p.121

[117] *Ibid.*

[118] *Storck v Germany* (2005) 43 EHRR 96 [74]; HRC '*General Comment No. 35: Article 9(Liberty and Security of Person)*' CCPR/C/GC/35 (Hereinafter 'GC.35')

[119] *De Wilde Ooms and Versyp v Belgium* (1971) 1 EHRR 373 [65]

[120] *Amuur v France* (1996) 22 EHRR 533 [50]

[121] *Saadi v UK* [2008] ECHR 80 [67]-[74]

[122] *Chahal v UK* [1996] ECHR 54 [129]

From its inception, Strasbourg's approach to immigration detention was highly deferential to state sovereignty.[123] The then-European Commission on Human Rights, held that detention did not have to be strictly necessary under Art.5(1)(f), provided that deportation proceedings were in place and being seriously pursued.[124]

This line of reasoning was adopted in the ECtHR's landmark case of *Chahal v UK*, concerning a foreign national terrorist suspect, who was detained for six years pending deportation. The applicant argued, *inter alia*, that the excessive duration of detention had ceased to conform with Article 5(1)'s legality requirement.[125] Finding no violation, however, the Court held that:

> 'Article 5 para.1(f) does not demand that...detention...be reasonably considered necessary, for example to prevent his committing an offence or fleeing...all that is required...is that "action is being taken with a view to deportation."'[126]

In rejecting the necessity test, the ECtHR affords the UK a wide margin of appreciation to detain in accordance with its immigration objectives. Indeed, as Cornelisse remarks, *'it would have been difficult for Article 5(1)(f) to be interpreted in a way which would have given the state any more discretion.'*[127] Proportionality is only applied to the extent that detention should not continue for an unreasonable length of time,[128] however prolonged detention is permissible where the state acts with due diligence.[129] The Court's endorsement of unnecessary indefinite detention is difficult to reconcile with Art.5's purpose of preventing arbitrariness.[130] As Johnston argues, the *'distinction between unnecessary indefinite detention and arbitrary detention can surely be little more than semantic.'*[131]

Saadi v UK concerns the second limb of Art.5(1)(f), *'to prevent unauthorised entry.'* The Court ruled that seven-day detention under the DFT for administrative convenience was not arbitrary, given that:

---

[123] Wilsher, p.140

[124] *Lynas v Switzerland* Application no.7317/75 (6.Oct.1967); *Caprino v United Kingdom* Application no.6871/75 (3 Mar.1978)

[125] *Chahal* [109]

[126] *Ibid.*[112]

[127] Cornelisse, p.295

[128] *Chahal* [113]

[129] *Ibid.*

[130] Cornelisse, p.101

[131] Johnston, C *'Indefinite Immigration Detention: Can it Be Justified?'*(2009) Journal of Immigration, Asylum and Nationality Law, 23(4) 351-364 p.360

> States enjoy an undeniable sovereign right to control aliens' entry into and residence in their territory. It is a necessary adjunct to this right that States are permitted to detain would-be immigrants who have applied for permission to enter, whether by way of asylum or not.'[132]

Strikingly, the Court opined that *'...until a State has "authorised" entry...any entry is "unauthorised"'* and is liable to detention under Article 5(1)(f).[133] This includes asylum seekers, clashing with interpretations of the Refugee Convention and HRC case law that consider an asylum seeker to be *'legally within the territory'* of a State once they claim asylum.[134] The Court's reasoning renders any 'unauthorised' foreign national liable to indefinite detention, regardless of necessity. While this appears to endorse discrimination on grounds of nationality, the Court maintains that any narrower construction would unduly curb *'the power of the State to exercise its undeniable right of control...'*[135] This political balance reproduces state-centric border control narratives, affording the state vast discretion to detain 'unauthorised' foreign nationals.

Proportionality is not completely missing from the judgment however, as the Court outlined four anti-arbitrariness criteria,[136] including that the *'length of the detention should not exceed that reasonably required for the purpose pursued.'*[137] Yet, this permits prolonged and indefinite detention, provided the state acts with due diligence.

In a powerful dissent, six judges condemned detention for administrative convenience as treating human beings as *'a means towards an end.'*[138] They questioned what constitutes a 'reasonable period'[139] and highlighted the disharmony of the majority's approach with other IHRL standards:

'Ultimately, are we now also to accept that Article 5 of the Convention...should afford a lower level of protection as regards asylum and immigration which, in social and human terms, are the most crucial issues facing us in the years to come? Is it a crime to be a foreigner? We do not think so.'[140]

---

132 *Saadi* [64]

133 *Ibid.*[65]

134 UNHCR ECC No.44; *A v Australia* Communication no.560/1993 (30 Ap. 1997)

135 *Saadi* [65]

136 [74]

137 *Ibid.*

138 *Ibid.* Joint partly dissenting opinion of Judges Rozakis, Tulkens, Kovler, Hajiyev, Spielmann and Hirvelä

139 *Ibid.*

140 *Ibid.*

That the dissenting judges reached such glaringly different conclusions demonstrates that interpreting Article 5(1)(f) as permitting unnecessary indefinite detention of non-nationals is not self-evident. Rather, it is a result of prioritising state objectives. As Costello remarks, '*Saadi* is a reflection of '*...the worst of Strasbourg's deference to statist approaches to migration control and status.*'[141]

There have been subsequent indications that the Court is softening its deferential approach to detention. In *Mikolenko v Estonia*,[142] the Court held that there must be a realistic prospect of removal where detention is with a view to deportation. Regarding particularly vulnerable persons,[143] the Court considers whether a less severe measure could have been adopted, incorporating a proportionality approach to Art.5(1)(f). In respect of children, it goes further in requiring child detention to be a measure of last resort.[144]

In *J.N. v UK*,[145] however, the Court reverted back to its deferential stance on indefinite detention. The applicant argued, *inter alia*, that the lack of foreseeability caused by the UK's lack of time limit fell short of the 'quality of law' requirement of Art.5(1).[146] The applicant also argued that the EU Returns Directive indicates European consensus that indefinite detention is inconsistent with human rights standards.[147] The Court, however, reiterated that Art.5(1)(f) does not require a maximum time limit while other procedural safeguards are in place,[148] the absence of which was only one of many factors that may determine legality.[149] Furthermore, the Court held that the Returns Directive is not the only system capable of complying with Art.5(1)(f).[150] The Court did find a violation of Art.5(1)(f), however, as the state had failed to act with due diligence.[151] Despite this, the Court is clear that it does not view the UK's practice of indefinite detention to be unlawful in principle under Art.5(1)(f). Thus, unnecessary and indefinite detention is permissible if deportation/removal proceedings are pursued with due diligence.

---

141 Costello, C '*The Human Rights of Migrants in European Law*'(2016) Oxford: Oxford University Press p.319

142 Application no.16944/03, 5 Jan.2006

143 *Yoh-Ekale Mwanje v Belgium* Application no.10486/10 20 Dec.2011 [124]

144 *Rahimi v Greece* Application no. 8687/08 5 Apr.2011 [109] *Popov v France* Applications nos.39472/07;39474/07, 19 Jan.2012 [91]

145 [2016] ECHR 434

146 *Ibid.*[59]

147 *Ibid.*[60]

148 *Ibid.*[90]

149 *Ibid.*

150 *Ibid.*[91]

151 *Ibid.*[107]-[108]

More recently, in *V.M. v UK,*[152] the Court held that the authorities had failed to act with due diligence in pursuing deportation proceedings, leading to an unreasonable period of detention under Art.5(1)(f). Importantly, it considered that the deterioration of the applicant's mental health entailed a *'heightened duty'* to act with due diligence and was a significant factor leading to the Court's conclusion that the state had failed in this duty.[153]However, citing *J.N*, it reaffirmed that a time limit on detention is unnecessary to fulfill the legality requirement of Art.5(1), thereby upholding the practice of indefinite detention in principle.

That the UK's system of indefinite detention does not necessarily violate Article 5 was again confirmed by the Court in an admissibility decision in April 2017, in *Arben Draga v United Kingdom.*[154] The applicant in the case also argued, *inter alia*, that the lack of time limit on detention fell short of the requirement of legality in Article 5(1), an argument that was, as in *J.N* and *V.M*, rejected by the Court. The Court opined that despite the lack of time limit or automated judicial review, the applicant was still able to challenge his detention at any time (an issue which will be discussed further in Section Three), and therefore the lack of time limit did not breach Article 5(1).

In permitting indefinite and unnecessary detention, the Court readily defers to state interests at the expense of individual rights. In respect of other types of detention, however, it takes a markedly different approach. For example, under Art.5(1)(e) (detention of *inter alia*, persons of unsound mind, alcoholics and vagrants), the Court held that deprivation of liberty is such a severe measure that it must be shown to have been necessary in the circumstances.[155] The denial of the same level of protection to immigration detainees suggests that their immigration status renders them less deserving of the right to liberty.

Prolonged detention may engage other ECHR rights, including Art.3 (prohibition of torture and inhuman and degrading treatment) or Art.8 (right to private/family life), which will be addressed in Section Four. The Court has accepted that prolonged detention can contribute to a violation of Art.3, as it may exacerbate the harmful effects of poor or unsuitable conditions.[156] Duration alone in adequate conditions, however, will

[152] Application no. 49734/12 1 Sep.2016

[153] *Ibid.*[96]-[99]

[154] *Arben Draga v United Kingdom* Application no. 33341/13 (25 April 2017)

[155] *Varbanov v Bulgaria* (2000) Reports 2000-X [46];*Winterwerp v Netherlands* [1979] ECHR 4 [39]

[156] *Dougoz v Greece* [2001] ECHR 213 [48]; *Popov* [100]-[103]

not breach Art.3.[157] Furthermore, in *Popov v France,*[158] the failure to consider alternative measures in circumstances of extreme vulnerability violated Art.8.[159]

Dembour contrasts Strasbourg's approach with the '*realism, humanism and thoroughness*'[160] in the Inter-American Court of Human Rights' (IACtHR) jurisprudence concerning immigration detention.[161] In *Vélez Loor v Panama,*[162] the IACtHR recognises that migrants are vulnerable to human rights abuse,[163] and while states have a margin of discretion to pursue immigration objectives, this must respect individual rights without discrimination.[164] As such, immigration detention should never be punitive, should be necessary and proportionate in the specific case, for the shortest period possible, and be used as a last resort.[165] Dembour describes this approach as '*pro-homine*' (biased towards the human being), conceiving the migrant first and foremost '*...as a human being in need of protection...*' whereas, in Strasbourg case law, '*...the migrant is first of all conceived as an alien subject to the control of the sovereign state.*'[166]

UN System

As noted by the dissenting judges in *Saadi*, the ECtHR's approach to Art. 5(1)(f) often fails to account for ICCPR jurisprudence. The right to liberty and security of person is enshrined in Art.9 ICCPR, considered of '*...profound importance...both for individuals and for society as a whole.*'[167] Unlike Art.5(1)(f) ECHR, Art.9 ICCPR does not expressly address immigration detention. The HRC has, however, clarified that Art. 9 applies to immigration detention.[168]

The starting point of difference between the HRC and ECtHR is that the HRC offers a more robust definition of 'arbitrariness', which '*...is not*

---

157 *A and Others v UK* (2009) 49 EHRR 29 [133]-[134]

158 *Popov v France* Applications nos. 39472/07 and 39474/07, 19 January 2012

159 *Ibid.* [119], [147]

160 Dembour p.385

161 Art.7 American Convention on Human Rights (Organization of American States, 'Pact of San Jose', Costa Rica, 22 November 1969)

162 *Vélez Loor v Panama*, Preliminary Objections, Merits, Reparations and Costs, Judgment (IACtHR)(23 Nov. 2010)

163 *Ibid.*[97]

164 *Ibid.*[100]

165 *Ibid.*[171]

166 Dembour p.8

167 GC.35 [2]

168 *Ibid.*[5]

to be equated with "against the law"' but also includes '*...elements of inappropriateness, injustice, lack of predictability and due process of law...this includes the principles of reasonableness and necessity.*'[169] It follows that unnecessary detention will likely be arbitrary.

In *A v Australia*, which concerned prolonged indefinite detention, the Committee held that:

> '...detention should not continue beyond the period for which the State can provide appropriate justification....there may be...factors particular to the individuals, such as the likelihood of absconding and lack of cooperation, which may justify detention for a period. Without such factors detention may be considered arbitrary, even if entry was illegal.'[170]

In a markedly different approach to the ECtHR in *Saadi*, the HRC held that the state cannot detain on grounds of illegal entry; there must exist a reason beyond that to justify detention. This recognises aliens' full right to liberty, as expressed in the HRC's General Comment (GC) 15.[171] Thus, detention is arbitrary where less invasive means are available to achieve the state's objectives.[172] Furthermore, there must be a realistic prospect of removal, thus the inability to effect removal cannot justify indefinite detention.[173] The HRC therefore requires that the decision to detain must be necessary and proportionate in the circumstances, on the assumption that everyone should be at liberty unless criminally convicted.[174] This seeks to more evenly balance objectives of immigration control against individual rights, recognising that immigration status does not in itself entail a lesser right to liberty.

It is likely that many instances of detention in the UK do not satisfy these requirements of necessity or proportionality, given the high rates of release. This has been recognised by the HRC, which has urged the UK to introduce a time limit, and to '*...ensure that detention is a measure of last resort and is justified as reasonable, necessary and proportionate...*'[175]

---

[169] *Fongum Gorji-Dinka v Cameroon* Communication no.1134/2002 (17 Mar.2005) [5.1]

[170] (cited n.112) [9.4]

[171] HRC '*General Comment no.15:The Position of Aliens Under the Covenant*' 27thsess(11 Apr.1986)-[7]

[172] *C v Australia* Communication no.900/1999 (28 Oct.2002)-[8.2]

[173] *M.M.M.et al. v Australia* Communication no.2136/201225-(28 Oct.2013)-[10.3]

[174] Wilsher, p.165

[175] HRC *Conc.obs* [21(a)]

The HRC has also held that detention must account for the mental health of detainees. In *F.J. et al v Australia,*[176] the HRC noted the *'negative impact that prolonged indefinite detention...can have on the mental health of detainees'*[177] and, as such, found that prolonged and indefinite detention was one of several factors that contributed to a violation of Art. 7 ICCPR, the prohibition of torture cruel, inhuman or degrading treatment.[178] This will be discussed further in Section Four.

The HRC's influence on UK practice is, however, diluted by the ICCPR's weak institutional enforcement mechanisms. Following the decision in *A v Australia,* for example, the Australian government refused to pay compensation to the author.[179]

These requirements of proportionality and necessity have also been incorporated into several other 'soft law' measures, including UNGA resolutions calling upon states to respect the rights of migrants, to end arbitrary detention and adopt alternatives.[180] Furthermore, the UNHCR detention guidelines provide that to avoid arbitrariness, detention must be necessary, reasonable and proportionate in the circumstances, and alternatives must be considered.[181]

The UN Working Group on Arbitrary Detention (WGAD), goes further, considering that:

> '...immigration detention should gradually be abolished...The criminalization of irregular migration exceeds the legitimate interests of States in...regulating irregular migration flows.'[182]

It continues that if there must be administrative detention, proportionality requires it to be the last resort.[183] This demonstrates the possibility of an interpretation of the right to liberty that positions the fundamental human rights of migrants above states' sovereign interests. Unfortunately, however, this interpretation has not been implemented by the UK.

---

176 Communication no.2233/2013(2 May 2016)

177 *F.J.*[10.6]

178 *Ibid.*

179 Wong, T '*Rights, Deportation, and Detention in the Age of Immigration Control'*(2015) Stanford: Stanford University Press p.49

180 see n.33

181 Guidelines 4.1-4.3

182 UNGA, *Report of the Working Group on Arbitrary* Detention'(2010) A/HRC/13/30 [58]-[59] (Hereinafter, 'WGAD Report')

183 *Ibid.*[59]

Conclusions

While the UK detains migrants indefinitely at great human and financial cost, high release rates indicate the futility of this practice. The ECtHR has recently found violations due to the UK's failure to act with due diligence, yet, by refusing to denounce indefinite immigration detention in principle and insist on necessity, it has failed to constrain this practice. In doing so, it sacrifices migrants' rights to liberty as a '*necessary adjunct*' to sovereign power. While the HRC offers more robust protection from arbitrary detention, it has not ruled out indefinite detention and its weak enforcement mechanisms have limited its impact.

Alternative approaches of the WGAD, IACtHR and dissenting Strasbourg judges show that a legal interpretation that protects the rights of detainees is possible. Yet, in light of the ECtHR judgments in *J.N.* and *V.M.*, it is clear that IHRL will not compel the UK government to adopt a time limit in the near future.

On the domestic political level, however, there are indications that the government is beginning to consider introducing a time limit. In response to the follow-up Shaw review, the current Home Secretary, Sajid Javid, departed from the usual government rhetoric in announcing, for the first time, that he will consider the practicalities of ending indefinite detention.[184] While far from a concrete commitment, this certainly represents a shift away from the usual hard line refusal to end indefinite detention. In addition, proposals to introduce a 28 day time limit have gained increased cross-party support as at mid-2019.[185] This suggests that the solution to ending indefinite detention in the UK will ultimately have to be found at the political level, and not from IHRL. While the ECtHR continues to prioritise sovereign territoriality, indefinite detention in the UK will continue until politics dictates otherwise.

Section Three: Barriers to Justice

Lack of procedural safeguards is a major contributor towards prolonged detention. Most immigration detainees have not been charged with or

[184] UK Home Office '*Home Secretary statement on immigration detention and Shaw report*' (2018) at: https://www.gov.uk/government/speeches/home-secretary-statement-on-immigration-detention-and-shaw-report

[185] Coates, S '*Labour and Tories back 28-day limit on immigrant detention*' (2019) The Times https://www.thetimes.co.uk/article/labour-and-tories-back-28-day-limit-on-immigrant-detention-qw3rrhh65; see also Immigration (Time Limit on Detention) Bill 2019 at: https://services.parliament.uk/bills/2017-19/immigrationtimelimitondetention.html

convicted of a crime,[186] yet enjoy lower procedural safeguards than criminal suspects. Inability to effectively challenge detention stems from lack of legal representation and other practical barriers, as well as the inadequacy of the bail process.[187] Insufficient judicial control has allowed detention to expand in size and duration, in accordance with political objectives and with little accountability.[188] This Section examines the efficacy of IHRL in protecting the rights of detainees in accessing justice.

Lack of Procedural Safeguards

Due process principles require a minimum standard of procedural safeguards for detainees. Detained criminal suspects must be released or charged after 24 hours in England and Wales (extendable to 96 hours) or 12 hours in Scotland (extendable to 24 hours)[189] and have the right to consult with a state-funded solicitor.[190] Terrorist suspects can be detained for 14 days without charge.[191] If charged, there is a statutory presumption in favour of bail[192] and a hearing in an independent and impartial court. A crime must be serious enough to warrant a custodial sentence.[193]

By contrast, immigration detention is an administrative measure, without court authorisation, that leads to indefinite detention. As noted, the presumption in favour of release is not adhered to in practice. Detainees must be given written reasons for their detention,[194] and for the decision to maintain detention in a Monthly Progress Report (MPR), again without judicial oversight.[195] Concerns raised over MPRs include that they are of poor quality, are cursory and fail to engage with detainees as human beings.[196] Moreover, MPRs often do not adequately consider impor-

---

186 Ashford, M '*Detained Without Trial: A Survery of Immigration Act Detention*'(1993) Joint Council for the Welfare of Immigrants p.xi

187 Bail for Immigration Detainees '*Submission to the APPG on Refugees and APPG on Migration's Parliamentary Inquiry into the Use of Immigration Detention in the UK*' (2014) p.1 (Hereinafter, 'BID APPG') at: http://www.biduk.org/sites/default/files/BID%20submission%20to%20detention%20inquiry_Access%20to%20legal%20advice%20in%20IRCs%20Sept%202014%20(2).pdf

188 Wilsher, p.351

189 s.41,s.44(3)(b) Police and Criminal Evidence Act (PACE) 1984; s.14-A Criminal Procedure (Scotland) Act (CPSA) 1995

190 PACE Code C s.3(3.1)(a)(ii); *Cadder v HM Advocate* [2010] UKSC 43

191 s.57 Protection of Freedoms Act 2012

192 s.4(1) Bail Act 1976; s.23B1 CPSA

193 *Hirst v UK (No 2)*[2005]ECHR 681 [77]

194 Rule 9 DCR

195 para.55.8 EIG

196 Shaw Review, pp.183-188

tant developments such as deterioration in mental health.[197] Importantly, the decision to maintain detention is insufficiently independent from the initial decision to detain, with both taken by the same executive body.

Access to Legal Representation

A detainee can challenge the legality of detention by way of judicial review, and/or *habeas corpus* proceedings in England and Wales. The detainee must instigate proceedings and navigate an immigration system of a '*nightmarish complexity,*'[198] often hampered by language and/or literacy barriers and limited knowledge of the system.[199] Such barriers render many detainees unfit to represent themselves.[200] While legal representation increases the likelihood of successfully challenging detention,[201] in a recent survey, Bail for Immigration Detainees (BID) found 54% were unrepresented and 25% had never had a lawyer.[202]

Many detainees rely upon legal aid surgeries in IRCs. Legal aid has been cut in recent years, and in 2012, the Legal Aid, Sentencing and Punishment of Offenders Act (LASPO) removed legal aid for the majority of non-asylum immigration matters in England and Wales. While detention-related matters and bail remain funded, detainees' immigration cases are not funded, unless they relate to asylum, human trafficking, certain types of judicial review or other limited exceptions.[203] This has resulted in detainees '*...yo-yoing in and out of detention as legal action secures release but fails to address the substantive issue leading to detention.*'[204] The Legal Aid Agency contracts a limited number of firms for IRCs, resulting

---

[197] Bosworth, p.186

[198] Dembour p.30

[199] *R (Iqbal) v SSHD* [2015] EWCA Civ 838 [49]

[200] *Farquharson (removal- proof of conduct)* [2013] UKUT 146 (IAC)

[201] BID APPG [26]

[202] BID, '*Legal advice Survey – Spring 2016*'(2016) at: http://www.biduk.org/sites/default/files/media/docs/Legal%20Advice%20Survey%20-%20Spring%202016_1.pdf (Hereinafter, 'BID Survey')

[203] UK Ministry of Justice '*Post-Implementation Review of Part 1 of the Legal Aid, Sentencing and Punishment of Offenders Act 2012 (LASPO)*' (2019) pp.55-56 at: https://assets.publishing.service.gov.uk/government/uploads/system/uploads/attachment_data/file/777038/post-implementation-review-of-part-1-of-laspo.pdf

[204] York, S '*The end of legal aid in immigration - a barrier to access to justice for migrants and a decline in the rule of law*'(2013) J.I.A.N.L.27(2), 106-138 p.108

in overstretched representatives, compromised quality of advice,[205]and delays for appointments.[206]

In Scotland, a number of cuts were made to legal aid in 2011. However, financial assistance for immigration matters currently remains more available in Scotland than in England and Wales, with funding available for advice and assistance, tribunal and court representation in immigration cases.[207] As a result, detainees are better represented in Scotland.[208]This can be contrasted with the decreasing number of detainees represented in England and Wales since LASPO.[209] It appears that the Scottish Government intends to maintain the scope of legal aid in Scotland in respect of immigration matters.[210] By contrast, following its recent review into LASPO and legal aid reforms, the UK Government has not indicated any intention to restore legal aid for immigration cases in England and Wales, beyond reinstating funding for unaccompanied minors.[211] The lack of legal aid funding for immigration matters is therefore of particular concern in England, where the majority of immigration

---

205 IMB '*Campsfield House Immigration Removal Centre Annual Report*'(2015) p.11 at: http://www.imb.org.uk/wp-content/uploads/2016/04/Campsfield-House-2015.pdf

206 HMIP '*Report on an Unannounced Inspection of Campsfield House Immigration Removal Centre*'(2014) p.26 at: https://www.justiceinspectorates.gov.uk/hmiprisons/wp-content/uploads/sites/4/2015/02/Campsfield-House-web-2014.pdf

207 Law Society of Scotland '*Inquiry into Immigration Detention*' (2018) pp. 5-6 at: https://www.lawscot.org.uk/media/361494/18-11-21-imm-inquiry-immigration-detention.pdf

208 HMIP '*Report on an Unannounced Inspection of Dungavel House Immigration Removal Centre*'(2015) p.27 at: https://www.justiceinspectorates.gov.uk/hmiprisons/wp-content/uploads/sites/4/2015/07/Dungavel-web-2015.pdf

209 BID APPG [17]

210 Law Society of Scotland '*Inquiry into Immigration Detention*' (2018) pp. 5-6 at: https://www.lawscot.org.uk/media/361494/18-11-21-imm-inquiry-immigration-detention.pdf and Evans, M '*Rethinking legal aid: an independent strategic review*' (2018) at: *https://www.gov.scot/binaries/content/documents/govscot/publications/factsheet/2018/02/rethinking-legal-aid-an-independent-strategic-review/documents/rethinking-legal-aid-independent-strategic-review-pdf/rethinking-legal-aid-independent-strategic-review-pdf/govscot:document/Rethinking%20Legal%20Aid%20-%20an%20independent%20strategic%20review.pdf*

211 UK Ministry of Justice '*Post-Implementation Review of Part 1 of the Legal Aid, Sentencing and Punishment of Offenders Act 2012 (LASPO)*' (2019) at: https://assets.publishing.service.gov.uk/government/uploads/system/uploads/attachment_data/file/777038/post-implementation-review-of-part-1-of-laspo.pdf

detainees are held. Further, even where funding may be available for detention cases, those ineligible for legal aid often still cannot afford enough private advice to be effective.[212]The restricted availability of legal aid therefore clearly presents risks of negative impacts in terms of access to justice for a large proportion of the immigration detainee population in the UK.[213]

Further barriers are faced by detainees with disabilities, trauma, mental illness and/or those in segregation, who often do not receive adequate assistance in contacting lawyers.[214] The struggle to find a lawyer is a common source of distress, and, compounded by indefinite/prolonged detention, can have a profound impact on welfare.[215]

Foreign National Ex-Offenders

97% of foreign national ex-offenders (FNO) are detained in prison under immigration powers at the end of their custodial sentence,[216] where the abovementioned barriers are exacerbated. As prisons do not provide the minimal safeguard of legal surgeries,[217] it is unsurprising that 78% of FNOs were unrepresented in BID's survey and many experience prolonged detention.[218] FNOs are routinely refused bail on grounds of risk of re-offending, and so are continually deprived of their liberty, despite having served their sentence.[219] Immigration detention is not part of the criminal justice system, and considering its lesser safeguards, should not be used punitively or to prevent crime.

---

212 APPG Inquiry p.6

213 Bail for Immigration Detainees '*Six-monthly survey reveals lack of legal representation for immigration detainees*' (2018) at: https://www.biduk.org/posts/429-six-monthly-survey-reveals-lack-of-legal-representation-for-immigration-detainees

214 BID APPG p.45

215 Bosworth, p.146

216 Bail for Immigration Detainees '*Liberty Deficit: Long-term detention and bail decision*-making'(2012) p.45 at: http://www.biduk.org/sites/default/files/BID%20report%20The%20Liberty%20Deficit%20December%202012_0.pdf (Hereinafter '*Liberty Deficit*')

217 *Liberty Deficit* p.9

218 *Ibid.*

219 Detention Action '*Detained Lives: the real cost of indefinite immigration detention*'(2009) p.6 at: http://detentionaction.org.uk/wordpress/wp-content/uploads/2011/10/Detained-Lives-report.pdf

Bail

It is important to emphasise that bail itself is a restriction of liberty, and entails review only of the detainee's suitability for temporary release with conditions, not the legality of detention.[220] For many, the abovementioned barriers render the bail process inaccessible,[221] especially as detainees must instigate bail proceedings, lacking knowledge of the process.[222]

In a positive development, the IA 2016 introduced automatic bail hearings after four months,[223] which was implemented in January 2018. This provision excludes FNOs and persons detained pending removal in the interests of national security – detainees which are typically detained for the longest periods.[224] Yet, it remains the case that four months in detention potentially without review is excessive, considering the negative impacts of much shorter periods.[225] In July 2018, in response to the critical follow-up Shaw Report, the government announced that it will pilot an additional bail referral after two months.[226] The pilot commenced in February 2019 and is ongoing as at mid-2019. Yet, automatic bail hearings still do not address fundamental shortcomings in accessing justice, including legal aid and access to legal representation, and do not allow the detainee to challenge the legality of detention.

Where detainees are allowed a bail hearing, the IA 2014 interfered with the independence of the bail process by imposing restrictions on the decision to grant bail, including refusal of repeat applications within 28 days without a material change in circumstances[227] and where removal

---

220 Clements, '*Bail Guidance for Judges Presiding Over Immigratihon and Asylum Hearings*' June 2012 First-Tier Tribunal (Immigration and Asylum Chamber) at: https://www.judiciary.gov.uk/wp-content/uploads/2014/07/bail-guidance-immigration-judges.pdf

221 EHRC

222 BID'*A nice judge on a good day: immigration bail and the right to liberty*'(2010) p.21 at: http://www.biduk.org/sites/default/files/AGoodJudgeREPORT.pdf

223 Sch.10 s.11

224 House of Commons, House of Lords, Joint Committee on Human Rights '*Immigration detention – Sixteenth Report of Session 2017-2019*' (2019) p. 27 at: https://publications.parliament.uk/pa/jt201719/jtselect/jtrights/1484/1484.pdf

225 See Section Two

226 UK Home Office, '*New commitments to tackling vulnerability in immigration detention announced*' (2018) at: https://www.gov.uk/government/news/new-commitments-to-tackling-vulnerability-in-immigration-detention-announced

227 s.7(6) IA 2014

directions have been set within two weeks.[228] The IA 2016 also prohibits the granting of bail within eight days of entry into the UK.[229]

It has been highlighted that those with language barriers or particular vulnerabilities, such as mental health issues, are at a significant disadvantage in terms of their ability to access both the bail system prior to the automatic hearing, as well as judicial review proceedings.[230] In particular, the Court of Appeal has highlighted the lack of provision of advocates for detainees with mental health conditions, who are less able to effectively assert their right to initiate the bail process or challenge the legality of their detention.[231]

Further problems limiting this remedy's effectiveness include issues with video-links and interpreters at bail hearings and insufficient time for lawyers to take instructions.[232] Of further concern is the reported tendency of bail judges to accept unsubstantiated arguments from the government regarding the likelihood of absconding or re-offending.[233]

Detained Fast Track

As noted in Section One, the Detained Fast Track system detained asylum seekers whose cases were viewed as quickly resolvable[234] but was suspended in 2015 following legal challenges over its lack of appropriate safeguards.[235] In reviewing the legality of the operation of the DFT, the High Court considered that independent, effective legal representation was '*...the crucial safeguard, the crucial ingredient for a fair hearing...*'[236]Yet, lawyers were frequently allocated to DFT cases without sufficient time to take proper instructions. While the Court identified

[228] *Ibid.* s.7(2)

[229] Sch 2 s.16(1) IA 2016

[230] House of Commons, House of Lords, Joint Committee on Human Rights '*Immigration detention – Sixteenth Report of Session 2017-2019*' (2019) p. 28 at: https://publications.parliament.uk/pa/jt201719/jtselect/jtrights/1484/1484.pdf

[231] *Ibid.* and *R (VC) v SSHD* [2018] EWCA Civ 57

[232] *Liberty Deficit* p.25

[233] *Ibid.* p.21

[234] UK Home Office '*Detained Fast Track Processes*' p.4 at: https://www.gov.uk/government/uploads/system/uploads/attachment_data/file/370322/Detained_Fast_Track_Processes_v6_0.pdf

[235] UK Home Office '*Written Statement made by: The Minister of State for Immigration (James Brokenshire)*' July 2015 at: http://www.parliament.uk/documents/commons-vote-office/July%202015/2%20July/6-Home-Asylum.pdf

[236] *Detention Action v SSHD* [2014] EWHC 2245 (Admin)[195]

other deficiencies, this was the decisive factor that lead to the finding that the DFT was operating unlawfully.[237]

International Human Rights Law

European Court of Human Rights

Due process principles are enshrined in Art.6 ECHR, which guarantees the right to a fair trial in the determination of civil rights/criminal charges and access to an independent court. In *Maaouia v France,*[238] however, the ECtHR held that Art.6 does not apply to decisions regarding the entry, stay and deportation of aliens due to the:

> '...substantial discretionary and public-order element in such decisions...even if they...have major repercussions on...private and family life, prospects of employment, financial position and the like.'[239]

The Court relied upon Art.1 Protocol 7 ECHR (procedural guarantees in administrative proceedings), despite the fact its Explanatory Report provides that it does not affect Art.6.[240] This approach fails to account for the severe impact of immigration/asylum decisions on the lives of those they concern, including that such decisions can lead to detention.

Art.5 ECHR is therefore of greater relevance in terms of procedural safeguards for immigration detainees. Art.5(1) contains the principle of legality, which demands a certain 'quality of law' that is accessible and foreseeable,[241] including effective remedies to challenge arbitrariness.[242] Art.5(2) requires individuals to be informed with reasons for detention, Art.5(4) guarantees the right to challenge detention and be released where detention is unlawful, and Art.5(5) contains a right to compensation for unlawful detention.

In *Chahal,* the Court distinguishes Article 5(1)(f) from Article 1(1)(c) (criminal procedural safeguards). Judge Pettiti disputes this in a partly dissenting judgment, emphasising that:

> '...The principle contained in Article 5...of immediately bringing a detained person before a court is intended to pro-

237 *ibid.* [220]

238 [2000] ECHR 455

239 *Ibid.* [40]

240 Explanatory Report on Protocol no.7 ECHR ETS 117 [7]

241 *Nasrulloyev v Russia,* Application no.656/06 (11 Oct.2007) [71]

242 *Louled Massoud v Malta* Application no.24340/08 (27 Jul.2010) [71]

tect liberty and not to serve as "cover" for detention which has not been justified by a criminal court.'[243]

The majority, however, make this distinction without explanation, as if self-evident that one category should be granted a higher protection of liberty than the other.

The ECtHR has held that where detention is indefinite, the necessity of procedural safeguards becomes decisive.[244] Furthermore, as the ECHR is '*...intended to guarantee rights that are not theoretical or illusory, but practical and effective...*', there must be a realistic possibility of accessing the remedy.[245]

Art 5(4) provides a *lex specialis* in relation to the more general requirements of Art.13 ECHR (right to an effective remedy).[246] The purpose of Art.5(4) is to guarantee detainees '*...the right to a judicial supervision of the lawfulness of the measure to which they are thereby subjected.*'[247] The review must have a judicial character,[248] should allow the affected individual to participate in the proceedings,[249] and should be accessible and effective in theory and practice.[250]

Art.5(4) places the burden of justifying detention on the government,[251] and so the purported tendency of bail judges to accept the government's unsubstantiated reasons for detention falls short of this requirement.

Art.5(1) and Art.5(4) clearly require an accessible remedy to review detention. As demonstrated, however, while detainees in the UK have the right to challenge their detention, several barriers render this difficult in practice. This was highlighted in *J.N.*, where the applicant highlighted the many barriers to accessing judicial remedies in the UK, including language barriers, lack of knowledge of the system and difficulty accessing legal aid.[252] The applicant argued that automatic independent judicial scrutiny of the legality of detention was important to fulfil the accessibility requirement of Art.5(1).[253]

243 *Chahal* Partly Dissenting Opinion of Judge Petiti
244 *Chahal* [71]
245 *Čonka v Belgium* Application no.51564/99 (5 Feb.2002)
246 *Jong, Baljet and van den Brink v Netherlands* (1986) 8 EHRR 20 [60]; *Chahal* [126]
247 *De Wilde* [76]
248 *Louled Massoud* [40]
249 *Weeks v UK* [1987] ECHR 3 [66]
250 *Muminov v Russia* Application no.42502/06 (11 Dec.2008) [113]
251 *Zamir v UK* (1983) 5 EHRR 242 [58]
252 *J.N.*[62]
253 *Ibid.*

The ECtHR, however, held that Art 5(1)(f) does not necessitate automatic judicial review of immigration detention, although the effectiveness of existing remedies was relevant in its overall assessment of arbitrariness.[254] The Court accepted that 'in principle' the UK system provided an effective remedy, as detainees can challenge the lawfulness of their detention at any time.[255] Despite its jurisprudence requiring accessibility, the Court sidestepped the argument that remedies were often inaccessible and ineffective in practice.[256] The Court relinquished the opportunity to use Art.5(4) to guarantee an equal standard of procedural safeguards for immigration detainees in the UK.[257] It upheld this finding in *V.M*,[258]and more recently again in *Arben Draga*, where the Court held that despite unautomated judicial review, the applicant was able to challenge his detention at any given time, again without regard to the practicality and accessibility of doing so.

Inter-American Court of Human Rights Comparison

By contrast, the IACtHR affords equal procedural safeguards to immigration detention and other deprivations of liberty. In an important opinion pronouncing the right to equality and non-discrimination as *jus cogens*,[259] the IACtHR held that:

'*...the right to due process of law must be recognized as one of the minimum guarantees that should be offered to any migrant, irrespective of his migratory status.*'[260]

In *Vélez Loor*, the IACtHR considered the *habeas corpus* remedy available to immigration detainees to be unsatisfactory as it was ineffective in practice.[261] The IACtHR emphasised the particular vulnerability of a detained alien who may not know the country's legal system, and must therefore be guaranteed'*...effective access to justice in equal terms.*'[262] This included the provision of legal aid where necessary.[263] The IACtHR places the principles of equality and non-discrimination at the heart of its reasoning, recognising the inherent vulnerability of the immigration detainee. As such, the burden is placed upon the state to

---

254 *J.N.*[94]

255 *Ibid.*[98]

256 *Ibid.*[100]

257 Dembour p.383

258 *V.M* [91]

259 *Advisory Opinion on Juridical Condition and Rights of the Undocumented Migrants*, OC-18/03 (IACtHR) 17 September 2003 [101]

260 *Ibid.* [73]

261 *Vélez Loor* [139]

262 *Ibid.*[132]

263 *Ibid.*

prove that its practices guarantee *'full procedural equality'* between aliens and citizens.[264] The ECtHR, by contrast, defers to state practice that affords migrants lesser procedural safeguards, simply because they are migrants.

The UN System

Unlike the ECtHR in *Maaouia*, the HRC has not definitively ruled out the application of Art.14 ICCPR (fair trial) to immigration cases.[265] However, in *Madafferi v Australia*, it referred to the ECtHR approach and held that an administrative decision to deny a visa does not amount to a 'suit at law' for the purposes of Art.14. This suggests that it may decline to consider other immigration-related matters – such as the decision to detain – under Art.14.

As noted, Art.9(1) ICCPR includes the principle of legality. Arts.9(2), 9(4) and 9(5) substantively reflect the equivalent provisions of Art.5(2), (4) and (5) ECHR.

Art.9(4) enshrines the principle of *habeas corpus*.[266] In *A v Australia*, the HRC held that Art.9(4) requires that review of detention is, '*...in its effects, real and not merely formal.*'[267] As such, a review of detention must ensure not only compliance with domestic law,[268] but with the requirements of reasonableness, proportionality and necessity under Art. 9(1).[269]

In addition, the BOP requires detainees to be given reasons for their detention and information on their rights in a language they understand, and free use of an interpreter where necessary.[270]

The HRC states that the decision to detain under immigration powers must be subject to periodic re-evaluation and judicial review.[271] Unlike criminal cases under Art.9(3), Art.9(4) does not require automatic review, and permits the measure to be initiated by the detainee.[272] Thus, like the ECtHR, the HRC considers that criminal cases are afforded higher safeguards than other deprivations of liberty. The WGAD, however, urges states to afford equal safeguards to immigration detainees, stating that detention must be judicially approved, subject to '*...automatic, regular*

---

264 *Ibid.*[143]

265 Cornelisse p.182

266 *Gavrilin v Belarus* Communication no.1342/2005 (28 Oct.2004) [7.4]

267 *A* [9.5]

268 *Baban v Australia* Communication no.1014/2001 (6 Aug.2003)

269 *Shams et al v Australia* Communication no.1255/2004 (11 Sep.2007)

270 Principle 14 BOP

271 GC.35 [12]

272 *Ibid.*[46]

and judicial, not only administrative, review of detention in each individual case.'[273]

Inaccessible remedies will also violate Art.9(4),[274] therefore detainees should be informed, in a language they understand, of their right to challenge the lawfulness of their detention.[275] Thus, the HRC acknowledges the practical barriers to justice that detainees may face. These barriers are also recognised by the Committee on the Elimination of Discrimination Against Women (CtEDAW), which stresses the importance of legal aid to enable women to effectively challenge administrative detention.[276]

In its concluding observations for the UK, the HRC has raised concerns over the operation of the DFT and urged the UK to provide '*...effective safeguards against arbitrariness and for effective access to justice, including to legal aid.'*[277] The HRC expressed further concerns over legal aid cuts in the UK and the negative impact on access to justice,[278] which has been echoed by the Committee for Economic Social and Cultural Rights (CESCR).[279]

In respect of FNOs, the HRC states that if a FNO has fully served their sentence, Arts.9 and 15 ICCPR prohibit a retroactive increase in sentence. Thus, a state may not impose detention that is equivalent to penal imprisonment under the guise of civil detention.[280] Furthermore, the WGAD has held the continued preventative detention of FNOs, without the usual criminal procedural safeguards, amounts to discrimination on grounds of citizenship, violating Art.26 ICCPR (equal protection before the law).[281]

The UN Special Rapporteur on the Human Rights of Migrants (SRHRM) has expressed concern over remedies that are initiated upon request of the migrant,[282] and has urged the UK to grant detainees all ju-

---

273 WGAD Report [61]

274 *A* [9.5]

275 GC.3555]

276 CtEDAW '*General recommendation No.33 on women's access to justice*'(2015) CEDAW/C/GC/33 [53]

277 HRC *Conc.obs* [xx]

278 *Ibid.*[21]

279 CESCR, '*Concluding observations on the sixth periodic report of the United Kingdom of Great Britain and Northern Ireland*'(2016) E/C.12/GBR/CO/6 [21](Hereinafter, 'CESCR *Conc.obs*')

280 GC.35 [21]

281 WGAD, *Abdi v United Kingdom of Great Britain and Northern Ireland* (2007) no.45/2006, A/HRC/7/4/Add.1at 40

282 Human Rights Council, '*Report of the Special Rapporteur on the human rights of migrants, Jorge Bustamante*' 25 February 2008 A/HRC/7/12 [46]

dicial guarantees, including keeping them informed of the status of their cases.[283]

These UN bodies have recognised barriers to justice for detainees, however, the HRC does not require the UK to introduce automatic judicial review of detention, which would most effectively guard against arbitrariness. While the SRHRM and WGAD have criticised remedies that depend upon initiation by detainees, the UK has not implemented these recommendations.

Conclusions

The IA 2016 entails a positive, albeit limited, development in introducing automatic bail hearings, gained through pressure from civil society and committed politicians. It appears that IHRL had less influence, given that the ECtHR permits the dilution of procedural rights for migrants. While detention may be described as 'criminalising' immigration, in another sense, its weak procedural safeguards indicate that it has not been criminalised enough.[284] Cornelisse argues that affording states discretion over procedural guarantees accords with traditional perceptions of the sovereign power to exclude,[285] reinforcing the territoriality of rights - that rights are for citizens, not humans. The approaches of the IACtHR and, increasingly, different UN bodies, demonstrate that this approach is not inevitable. Unfortunately, however, it is the ECtHR approach that continues to carry most influence in the UK.

Section Four: Heightened Vulnerabilities

All immigration detainees are vulnerable to an extent, given their unequal power relationship with the detaining authorities. Vulnerability can be conceptualised as *'...a concentric circle of personal (internal), social and environmental (external) factors that may strengthen or weaken an individual's personal integrity.'*[286]The detainee population consists of a wide diversity of intersecting vulnerabilities that affects ability to cope

[283] UNGA Human Rights Council, '*Report of the Special Rapporteur on the human rights of migrants, Jorge Bustamante: Mission to the United Kingdom of Great Britain and Northern Ireland*' (2010) A/HRC/14/30/Add. 3

[284] Wilsher, p.168

[285] Cornelisse, p.181

[286] JRS, p.90

with detention, as confirmed by the Shaw Review. This Section assesses the role of IHRL in protecting the most vulnerable detainees.

Domestic Policy

Prior to the Shaw Review, para.55.10 EIG stated that the following groups were usually considered suitable for detention only in very exceptional circumstances:

· Unaccompanied children under age 10,

· The elderly, especially where supervision cannot be satisfactorily managed within detention;

· Pregnant women;

· Those with serious medical conditions, mental illness or disabilities which cannot be satisfactorily managed within detention;

· Identified victims of torture; and

· Identified victims of trafficking.

Age, pregnancy, disability and sexual orientation are also amongst the protected characteristics under the Equality Act 2010,[287] which requires a public authority to eliminate discrimination against protected persons.[288]

Despite this policy, vulnerable persons falling within - and outwith - these categories were frequently detained. As will be discussed below, the above policy was replaced by the Home Office's '*Adults at Risk*' policy[289] in 2016, following the Shaw Review.

Inadequacies in Healthcare

Medical Justice emphasises that due to past or present trauma, detainees have complex health needs. [290] Detainees must receive a medical examination within 24 hours of detention.[291] However, healthcare is of poor quality, with '*...short consultations, late screenings, poor use of inter-*

---

[287] s.4

[288] s.149

[289] UK Home Office, '*Immigration Act 2016: Guidance on adults at risk in immigration detention*'(2016) at: https://www.gov.uk/government/uploads/system/uploads/attachment_data/file/547519/Adults_at_Risk_August_2016.pdf

[290] Medical Justice (MJ) '*Healthcare in Detention: Written Evidence Submitted by Medical Justice to the Shaw Review*'(2015) p.1 at: http://www.medicaljustice.org.uk/wp-content/uploads/2016/04/althcareinDetention-SummarybyMedicalJusticeforShawReview.pdf; (Hereinafter 'MJ Shaw Review')

[291] Rule.34 DCR

preters, poor clinical assessments, and lack of adherence to clinical protocols.'[292]

Mental illness is prevalent in, and often exacerbated by, detention. Pre-existing trauma causes significant mental deterioration in detention[293] and prevalent forms of mental illness include depression, anxiety and Post Traumatic Stress Disorder (PTSD).[294] These vulnerabilities can lead to self-harm and suicide. In IRCs in 2017, there were six suicides and 528 incidents of serious self-harm, an alarming increase from the already shocking three suicides and 341 serious self-harm incidents in 2016.[295] Appallingly, most recent figures released by the government via a Freedom of Information request indicate that at least two people in detention attempt suicide each day.[296] Yet, mental healthcare in detention centres is especially poor,[297] with accusations of a 'culture of disbelief' amongst healthcare staff.[298] The presumption against detaining the mentally ill was overturned following the addition of the phrase '*which cannot be satisfactorily managed in detention'* to para.55.10 in 2010.[299]The Shaw Review recommends that this be reversed,[300] and those with PTSD should not be detained.[301]

In terms of identifying vulnerable detainees, Rule 35 DCR (R35) requires a medical practitioner to report to the detaining authority where they are concerned that the detainee has a special illness, condition or is a torture victim. Problems with R35 are widespread, including insufficient staff training in recognising vulnerability, attitudinal problems and low

---

292 MJ Shaw Review, p.1

293 Shaw Review, p.305

294 *Ibid.*p.305

295 *'End the inhumanity of immigration detention'* (2018) Guardian at: https://www.theguardian.com/uk-news/2018/mar/15/end-the-inhumanity-of-immigration-detention

296 Taylor, D, Walker, P and Grierson, J *'Revealed: two suicide attempts every day in UK deportation centres'* (2018) Guardian at: https://www.theguardian.com/uk-news/2018/oct/11/revealed-two-suicide-attempts-every-day-uk-deportation-detention-centres

297 APPG Inquiry, p.56

298 Tsangarides, N *'The Second Torture: the Immigration Detention of Torture Survivors'*(2012) MJ p.88 at: http://www.medicaljustice.org.uk/wp-content/uploads/2016/03/the-second-torture-full-version.pdf (Hereinafter 'Tsangarides')

299 Royal College of Psychiatrists, *'Position Statement on detention of people with mental disorders in Immigration Removal Centres'*(2015) p.1 at: http://www.rcpsych.ac.uk/pdf/Satisfactory%20Treatment%20in%20Detention%20document%20December%202015%20edit.pdf

300 Shaw Review, Recommendation 11

301 *Ibid.*Recommendation 12

understanding of its purpose.[302] Medical Justice report that 65% of Home Office caseowners do not respond appropriately to R35 reports,[303] while HMIP observes that the R35 process is not working consistently well at any IRC.[304] This has resulted in the detention of many vulnerable persons. Similar concerns around the failure to identify and prevent the detention of vulnerable detainees were raised over the operation of the DFT. The UN Special Rapporteur on violence against women, its causes and consequences observed that the speed of the DTF process failed to identify vulnerable persons such as survivors of torture, sexual violence and trafficking.[305]

In addition to the prison-like resemblance of IRCs, which may trigger past trauma, another punitive quality of detention is the use of segregation. Rules 40 and 42 DCR allow segregation for safety reasons or for '*refractory or violent*' individuals. There is evidence that segregation is misused, including for mentally ill detainees.[306] In the Verne IRC, for example, a mentally ill detainee was segregated for 70 days, likely exacerbating his condition.[307] Liberty highlights that a Home Office DSO on Removal from Association[308] risks allowing segregation as an arbitrary punishment for disobedience, without any formal disciplinary process.[309] In addition, it allows for segregation to manage risk of suicide and self-

---

302 Tsangarides p.30

303 *Ibid.*

304 HMIP '*Annual Report 2015-2016*' (2016) p.71 at: https://www.gov.uk/government/uploads/system/uploads/attachment_data/file/538854/hmip-annual-report.pdf

305 UNGA, Human Rights Council, '*Report of the Special Rapporteur on violence against women, its causes and consequences, Rashida Manjoo: Mission to the United Kingdom of Great Britain and Northern Ireland*'(2015) A/HRC/29/27/Add.2 [42] (Hereinafter, 'SRVAW')

306 MJ '*A Secret Punishment: The Misuse of Segregation in Immigration Detention*'(2015) at: http://www.medicaljustice.org.uk/wpcontent/uploads/2016/05/MJ_Segregation_report_WEB_version_04_11_15-1.pdf

307 IMB '*Annual Report of the Board for The Verne Immigration Removal Centre*'(2015) p.12 at: http://www.imb.org.uk/wp-content/uploads/2016/05/The-Verne-2015.pdf

308 UK Home Office, '*Detention Services Order 02/2017 Removal from Association (Detention Centre Rule 40) and Temporary Confinement (Detention Centre Rule 42)*' (2017) at: https://assets.publishing.service.gov.uk/government/uploads/system/uploads/attachment_data/file/630008/DSO_02_2017_-_Rule_40_and_42.pdf

309 Liberty, '*Liberty's response to the draft Home Office DSO on Removal from Association and Temporary Confinement*' (2016) [9] at: https://www.liberty-human-rights.org.uk/sites/default/files/Liberty's%20Response%20to%20the%20DSO%20on%20Removal%20from%20Association%20and%20Temporary%20Confinement.pdf

harm.[310] This raises serious concerns over accountability and detainee welfare.

Gendering Detention

Detention produces and reproduces gendered harms by exacerbating past gender-based trauma, such as sexual violence, and by overlooking the gender-specific needs of detainees. The Shaw review recommends that survivors of gender-based violence (GBV) should not be detained.[311] While gendered experiences do not necessarily equate with women's experiences, the detention of vulnerable women at Yarl's Wood IRC has earned its description as a *'place of national concern.'*[312] 45% of detainees said they felt unsafe there,[313] with invasion of female detainees' privacy by male staff a recurring concern.[314] An independent review into concerns surrounding Yarl's Wood IRC commissioned by Serco plc, the private company subcontracted by the Home Office to manage Yarl's Wood, found that cutting costs had been a significant objective of the detention centre management, which involved reducing staff numbers.[315] Resulting severe staff shortages of female staff in particular at Yarl's Wood, is a damaging consequence of Serco plc's cost-cutting objectives.

HMIP found safeguarding procedures were inadequate and vulnerable persons continued to be detained, such as those displaying clear trafficking indicators.[316] Furthermore, 99 pregnant women were detained in 2014, with only nine removed from the UK.[317] Detention is particularly harmful for pregnant women due to the lower standard/accessibility of antenatal care and the impact of stress on the mother and foetus.[318] The

---

310 *Ibid.*[16] and DSO 02/2017 [24]-[25]

311 Shaw Review Recommendation 9

312 HMIP YW p.7

313 *Ibid* p.5

314 Women for Refugee Women *'I Am Human: Refugee Women's Experiences of Detention in the UK'*(2015) p.5 at: http://www.refugeewomen.co.uk/2016/wp-content/uploads/2016/02/WRW_IamHuman_report-for-web.pdf

315 Lampard, K and Marsden, E *'Independent investigation into concerns about Yarl's Wood immigration removal centre'*(2016) Verita p.64 at: https://www.verita.net/wp-content/uploads/2016/04/Independent-investigation-into-concerns-about-Yarls-Wood-immigration-removal-centre-Serco-plc-Kate-Lampard-Ed-Marsden-January-2016-1.pdf

316 HMIP YW p.29

317 *ibid.*p.6

318 MJ *'Expecting Change: The case for ending the detention of pregnant women'*(2013) at: http://www.medicaljustice.org.uk/wp-content/uploads/2016/03/expectingchange.pdf

IA 2016 introduced a welcome safeguard of a 72 hour time limit (extendable to seven days) on detaining pregnant women.[319] However, this falls short of the total ban advocated by the Shaw Review. [320] The Home Office also introduced a policy specifically addressing the detention of pregnant women in July 2016, which states:

> 'The enforced removal of a pregnant woman must only be pursued where it can be achieved safely and there is no suggestion that her baby is due before the planned removal date.'[321]

The Home Office's rationale for detaining pregnant women at all remains dubious, especially considering the grave risk detention places upon the health of the mother and baby, compared with the low removal rates of pregnant women.[322]

LGBTQI+ Detainees

While the government recognises the vulnerability of trans and intersex persons in detention,[323] in practice, the segregation of transgender/transsexual detainees amounts to a further gendered harm in detention.[324] The Shaw review expressed concern that IRCs are unable to provide an appropriate, safe and supportive environment for trans people[325] and as such recommends a presumption against detention of 'transsexual persons.' [326]

The Government does not currently recognise lesbian, gay, bi-sexual and queer people as particularly vulnerable in detention.[327] This is despite the fact that evidence indicates that lesbian, gay, bisexual, transgender, queer and intersex + (LGBTQI+) detainees commonly face bullying, abuse and harassment at the hands of other detainees and members of

---

[319] s.60

[320] HL Deb 10 May 2016 vol 771 c1668

[321] UK Home Office, '*Chapter 55a Detention of pregnant women*' (2018) at: https://assets.publishing.service.gov.uk/government/uploads/system/uploads/attachment_data/file/653012/Chapter_55a_Detention_of_pregnant_women_v1.pdf

[322] Detention Forum p.31

[323] UK Home Office '*Adults at Risk in Detention*' (2019) p.12 at: https://assets.publishing.service.gov.uk/government/uploads/system/uploads/attachment_data/file/784634/adults-at-risk-policy-v5.0ext.pdf

[324] Shaw Review p.50

[325] Shaw Review p.90

[326] *Ibid.* Recommendation 14

[327] House of Commons Home Affairs Committee '*Immigration Detention - Fourteenth Report of Session 2017-2019*' (2019) para.48 at: https://publications.parliament.uk/pa/cm201719/cmselect/cmhaff/913/913.pdf

detention centre staff.[328] As reported by Stonewall and the UK Lesbian and Gay Immigration Group, this creates a culture of intimidation for LGBTQI+ detainees who are reluctant to disclose such abuse as they are not confident they will receive support, or worse, will face repercussions.[329] Discouragingly, HMIP has observed a lack of targeted support for LGBTQI+ detainees generally.[330]

Allegations of Abuse

A Channel 4 News exposé in 2015 alleged instances of sexual abuse against detainees in Yarl's Wood and recorded staff making racist and sexist comments about detainees.[331] An investigation commissioned by Serco plc, concluded that misconduct was not widespread.[332] Alarmingly, the UN Special Rapporteur on Violence Against Women reported that the government prevented her from inspecting Yarl's Wood.[333] Further reports indicate that the government has refused to disclose information regarding sexual assault in Yarl's Wood so as not to '*...prejudice the commercial interests*' of its management.[334] Allegations of excessive use of force by detention staff outside of Yarl's Wood have also been made[335] and there remains a lack of accountability over such incidents. These disturbing allegations suggest that the government is prioritising commercial interests over the welfare of vulnerable detainees, forgoing transparency and accountability.

More recently, an uncover BBC Panorama report revealed shocking footage of detainees in Brook House IRC being subjected to racism, threats and physical abuse by G4S plc staff, as well as other alarming

328 Shaw Review p.94; and Stonewall and UK Lesbian & Gay Immigration Group '*No Safe Refuge: Experiences of LGBT Asylum Seekers in Detention*' (2016) p.19 at: https://www.stonewall.org.uk/system/files/no_safe_refuge.pdf

329 *Ibid.*

330 HMIP YW p.42

331 Channel 4 News '*Yarl's Wood: undercover in the secretive immigration centre*' (2015) at: http://www.channel4.com/news/yarls-wood-immigration-removal-detention-centre-investigation

332 Verita report p.12

333 SRVAW [29]

334 Fenton, S '*Home Office refuses to reveal whether women in Yarl's Wood have been raped in case it 'damages the commercial interests' of companies*' (2016) Independent at: http://www.independent.co.uk/news/uk/politics/home-office-refusing-to-reveal-whether-women-in-yarls-wood-have-been-raped-to-protect-the-commercial-a7077736.html

335 MJ '*Outsourcing Abuse*'(2008) at: http://www.medicaljustice.org.uk/wp-content/uploads/2016/03/outsourcing-abuse.pdf

practices, including staff falsifying detainee medical records.[336] The footage prompted both an independent inquiry into the treatment of detainees at Brook House, as well as a broader inquiry to assess the extent to which such issues are systemic across the detention estate.[337] A G4S commissioned review of Brook House reported concerns with the G4S whistleblowing procedure and that staff who had challenged abusive behavior by colleagues had been subjected to bullying and victimisation.[338] Despite these widespread concerns about G4S's management of Brook House, the House of Commons Home Affairs Committee reports that G4S has made profits from running Brook House beyond what was agreed in its contract with the Home Office.[339] The ability of a private company to maximise profit while failing to safeguard vulnerable detainees from the abuse of its own staff speaks to the risks presented by the privitisation of detention centres and is suggestive of an accountability deficit in the government's management of publicly funded contracts.

The Home Affairs Committee also highlights that the abuse of detainees at Brook House is not the first of its kind.[340] Yet, due to barriers discussed in Section Three, most detainees cannot challenge abuse through channels outside internal complaints procedures, which are often futile.[341]

Disability and Age

A further example of detention contrary to government policy includes detainees with physical disabilities in Heathrow and Harmondsworth

---

336 BBC Panorama, *'Undercover: Britain's Immigration Secrets'* (2017) at: https://www.bbc.co.uk/programmes/b094mhsn

337 McKinney, Conor James *'Home Affairs Committee probes "systemic" problems with immigration detention'* (2018) Free Movement at: https://www.freemovement.org.uk/home-affairs-committee-probes-systemic-problems-in-immigration-detention/

338 House of Commons Home Affairs Committee *'Immigration Detention: Fourteenth Report of Session 2017-2019'* (2019) para.254 at: https://publications.parliament.uk/pa/cm201719/cmselect/cmhaff/913/913.pdf

339 *Ibid.* para.273

340 *Ibid.* para.255

341 *Ibid.* pp.16-18

IRCs, who struggle to access basic facilities. The Heathrow IMB added that the resulting '*...indignity caused can border on the inhumane.*'[342]

In the year ending June 2016, 117 children entered detention - despite the government's pledge to end child detention in 2010.[343] The government has been accused of breaking this promise after announcing the closure of Cedars family pre-departure accommodation, placing children back into prison-like Tinsley House IRC.[344] Moreover, the detention and subsequent death of an 84-year-old suffering from Alzheimer's disease, who was declared unfit for detention, was deemed a '*tragic indictment of the system*' and highlighted inadequacies in the R35 process, risk assessments and staff training.[345]

Policy Developments

Detention Forum argues that the category-based approach in para.55.10 excluded persons that defy neat categorisation.[346] It also lacked intersectionality and overlooked vulnerabilities such as sexuality or GBV. Instead, Detention Forum advocates a vulnerability assessment tool that monitors personal, social and environmental factors (the concentric circle) that may change over time,[347] as part of an approach that favours community-based alternatives.

Following the initial Shaw Review, the government issued new guidance on the detention of adults 'at-risk', in accordance with s.59 IA 2016

342 IMB '*Annual Report: Heathrow Immigration Removal Centre*'(2015) p.9 at: http://www.imb.org.uk/wp-content/uploads/2016/05/Heathrow-IRC-2015.pdf; IMB '*Annual Report: Harmondsworth Immigration Removal Centre*'(2014) p.7 at: http://www.imb.org.uk/wp-content/uploads/2015/04/Harmondsworth-IMB-Annual-Report-2014.pdf

343 Detention Statistics

344 Stone, J '*Government accused of scrapping pledge to end child detention in prison-style immigration removal centres*' (2016) Independent at: http://www.independent.co.uk/news/uk/politics/child-detention-immigration-centres-scrapped-broken-promise-tinsley-house-cedars-barnados-home-a7149981.html

345 Newcomen, N '*Investigation into the death of a man on 10 February 2013 while a detainee at Harmondsworth Immigration Removal Centre*'(2015) at: http://www.ppo.gov.uk/wp-content/uploads/2015/10/H176-13-Death-of-a-male-detainee-in-hospital_Harmondsworth-IRC_10.02.13_Nat.pdf#view=FitH

346 Detention Forum '*Rethinking 'Vulnerability' in Detention: a Crisis of Harm*'(2015) p.53 at: http://detentionforum.org.uk/wp-content/uploads/2015/07/rethinkingvulnerability_8july.pdf

347 *Ibid.*

(Adults at Risk Policy),[348] which provides for individualised risk assessment as opposed to a category approach[349] and recognises a wider range of vulnerabilities, including victims of sexual violence, PTSD, transsexual and intersex persons.[350] It is concerning, however, that the guidance states that '*it will remain appropriate to detain individuals at risk if...necessary in order to remove them.*'[351] This dilutes the former EIG policy of detaining vulnerable persons in 'very exceptional' circumstances. As such, the policy has been criticised for inappropriately balancing vulnerability factors against 'immigration factors.'[352] Furthermore, the Adults at Risk Policy initially adopted a narrow definition of torture as only including torture inflicted by state actors, which was held by High Court to be unlawful. As a result of this narrow definition, torture survivors were unlawfully detained and, individuals excluded '*... whose experiences of the infliction of severe pain and suffering may indeed make them particularly vulnerable to harm in detention.*'[353] As a result, the government has revised the definition, implemented in July 2018.

The follow-up Shaw review highlighted major concerns surrounding the continued detention of vulnerable people. Shaw considers that while the Adults at Risk Policy represents a '*genuine focus on vulnerability*',[354] each of the IRC managers interviewed considered that the policy has made 'no difference' to the number of vulnerable people detained, and, in some cases, the detention of vulnerable people is actually increasing.[355] Shaw concluded that it is not clear that the policy has yet made a significant difference to the number of vulnerable people detained, and requires revision in order to meet its objectives.[356]

International Human Rights Law

Given the diversity of these issues, there are several IHRL instruments that may protect vulnerable individuals from detention.

---

[348] UK Home Office, '*Immigration Act 2016: Guidance on adults at risk in immigration detention*'(2016) at: https://www.gov.uk/government/uploads/system/uploads/attachment_data/file/547519/Adults_at_Risk_August_2016.pdf

[349] *Ibid.*[2]

[350] *Ibid.*[11]

[351] *Ibid.*[3]

[352] Follow-up Shaw Review p.4

[353] *Medical Justice & Ors v SSHD* [2017] EWHC 2461 (Admin) [154]

[354] Follow-up Shaw Review p.xii

[355] *Ibid.* p.viii

[356] *Ibid.* p.xii

European Court of Human Rights

Detention contrary to the EIG is unlawful[357] and violates the legality requirement of Art.5(1) ECHR.[358] Furthermore, Art.5(1) requires a sufficient relationship between the conditions and purpose of detention,[359] including suitable conditions for extremely vulnerable detainees.[360] As noted, while detention need not be necessary under Art.5(1),[361] in cases of particular vulnerability, the consideration of less severe measures will be relevant in determining whether detention is closely connected to its purpose.[362] In *V.M*, despite the applicant's deterioration in mental health, the Court found that detention was sufficiently connected to its purpose, as the applicant had not been detained under Art.5(1)(f), not Art.5(1)(e).[363] However, as noted, the ECtHR's ruling in *V.M.* is important in placing a '*heightened duty*' of due diligence on the state under Art.5(1)(f) in cases of deterioration in mental health caused by detention.[364] The applicant's deterioration in mental health, which led to her attempting suicide and self-harming, was a key factor leading to the finding a violation of Art.5(1)(f) in this case.[365]

The detention of vulnerable individuals may also violate Art.3 ECHR, which prohibits torture, inhuman and degrading treatment. The prohibition of torture is absolute,[366] indicated by its *jus cogens* status.[367] Art.3 requires ill-treatment to reach a minimum threshold of severity, dependent on the circumstances, including the duration of treatment, its physical and mental effects and characteristics of the victim.[368]

Art.3 entails negative and positive obligations to refrain from and prevent ill-treatment.[369] In *Kudła v Poland*, the ECtHR held that detention conditions must respect human dignity, must not lead to distress surpassing that inherent in detention, and must protect detainee welfare through,

---

357 para.55.1.1 EIG

358 *AMM (A Child) v SSHD* [2012] EWHC 2567 (QB)

359 *Aerts v Belgium* (2000) 29 EHRR 50 [46]

360 *Mubilanzila Mayeka and Kaniki Mitunga v Belgium* Application no. 13178/03 (12 Oct.2006) [102]-[103]; *Popov* [91]

361 *Chahal*

362 *Mwanje; Popov*

363 *V.M.* [93]

364 *Ibid.*[96]

365 *Ibid.*[99]

366 Art.15 ECHR; *Soering v UK* [1989] 11 EHRR 439 [88]

367 *Prosecutor v Furundzija* (IT-95-17/1-T) ICTY Trial Chamber (10 Dec. 1998) [153]–[157]

368 *Ireland v UK* [1978] ECHR 1[162]

369 *Slimani v France* (2006) 43 EHRR 49

inter alia, providing medical assistance.[370] In *Pretty v UK*, the Court held that naturally occurring illness may fall under Art.3 where it risks being exacerbated by detention.[371] Inadequate mental healthcare may violate Art.3, regardless of whether the affected person can prove resulting harm.[372] Failure to take reasonable steps to protect detainees from self-harm or suicide may also breach Art.2 ECHR (right to life).[373] In *V.M.*, the applicant's complaint under Art.3 (or Art.8) was inadmissible as it had not been raised before the domestic courts.[374]

Art.3 entails a positive obligation on the state to ascertain all relevant facts where it appears the individual may be a victim of torture.[375] Thus, the inadequacy of the R35 process may breach Art.3 where it fails to identify torture victims.

The ECtHR has held that segregation does not itself amount to inhuman treatment or punishment.[376] Whether segregation engages Art.3 depends on the particular conditions, stringency of the measure, its duration, the objective pursued and the effects on the person concerned.[377] The abovementioned incident at the Verne, for example, may engage Art. 3, given the prolonged nature of the treatment (70 days), the detainee's vulnerability and the resulting deterioration in mental health.[378]

Furthermore, unnecessary use of force against a detainee diminishes human dignity, contrary to Art.3.[379] Rape of a detainee by a state official is an especially grave form of ill-treatment, given the offender's ability to exploit their victim's vulnerability.[380]

The UK's failure to safeguard detainee welfare, the poor healthcare provision, failings of the R35 process in screening vulnerability, misuse of segregation and allegations of abuse by detention staff all may engage Art.3. However, ECtHR jurisprudence is clear that the suffering endured must meet a minimum threshold of severity in order to constitute a violation. This would have to be determined by individual case.

Due to the absolute nature of Art.3, the ECtHR refrains from adopting the sovereignty-focused approach seen in the previous Sections. In *M.S.S. v Belgium and Greece*, the Court declined to factor in states' concerns over increasing migration in determining their Art.3 obligations in

---

370 *Kudła v Poland* [2000] ECHR 512 [94]
371 (2002) 35 EHRR 1 [52]
372 *Keenan v UK* [2001] ECHR 242
373 *Ibid.*[89]-[99]
374 *V.M* [104]-[106]
375 *R.C. v Sweden* Application no.41827/07 (9 Mar.2010) [53]
376 *Öcalan v Turkey* [2005] ECHR 282
377 *Rohde v Denmark* (2005) 43 EHRR 325
378 *Keenan*
379 *Keenan* [131]
380 *Aydin v Turkey* [1997] ECHR 75

respect of detention conditions.[381] Similarly, in *Mayeka & Mitunga v Belgium*, the Court held that a five-year old unaccompanied child's '*...extremely vulnerable situation takes precedence over considerations relating to [her] status as an illegal immigrant.*'[382] This '*child first, migrant second*'[383] approach differs from the Court's Art.5(1)(f) approach, which is more akin to migrant first, human second.

The High Court has recently found five Art.3 violations concerning the immigration detention of the mentally ill.[384] In *R (BA) v SSHD*, the Court highlighted the '*deplorable failure*' by those responsible for *BA*'s detention to recognise the nature and extent of his mental illness,[385] holding that there had been a '*...combination of bureaucratic inertia...*' and '*....a callous indifference to BA's plight...*'[386]

In *R (S) v SSHD*, the detaining authority had justified the continued detention of S on grounds of risk of re-offending/absconding. The High Court held that this failed to consider the harmful effects of detention on S's mental health, which deteriorated in detention.[387] Citing *Pretty*, the Court considered this a '*sufficiently extreme case*' under Art.3[388] In finding a violation of Art.3, the Court held that detention exacerbated S's mental condition through debasement, humiliation and a '*...serious lack of respect for his human dignity...*[389]

In *R (HA (Nigeria)) v SSHD*, in addition to finding a violation of Art.3 as a result of a combination of acts and omissions in respect of a mentally ill detainee,[390] the Court declared the reformulation of the Home Office policy, outlined above, unlawful.

Johnson identifies patterns across these cases that '*may be symptomatic of underlying systemic failings.*'[391] Recurring themes were '*bureaucratic inertia*', poor healthcare and low quality MPRs. Common patterns in MPRs were uninformed decision-making and failure to engage with para.55.10's exceptionality test.[392]

---

381 (2011) 53 EHRR 2 [223]
382 *Mitunga* [55]
383 Dembour p.388
384 *R(S) v SSHD* [2011]EWHC 2120(Admin); *R(BA)*,n66; *R(HA (Nigeria))* v SSHD [2012]EWHC 979(Admin); *R(D) v SSHD* [2012]EWHC 2501(Admin); *R (MD) v SSHD* [2014] EWHC 2249 (Admin)
385 *R(BA* [236]
386 *Ibid.*[237]
387 *R(S)*[95]
388 *Ibid.*[192]
389 *Ibid.*[212]
390 *R(HA(Nigeria))*[181]
391 Shaw Review p.296
392 *Ibid.*p.298

For cases meeting the high threshold, the domestic courts have invoked IHRL in order to protect and compensate particularly vulnerable detainees. The effect of these judgments on practice remains questionable, considering these violations reoccurred over a three-year period and many of these issues were recently identified by the Shaw Review.

Many cases of ill-treatment, even if unlawful, do not meet the Art.3 threshold.[393] It may nonetheless breach the right to family and private life in Art.8 ECHR.[394] Art.8 is a qualified right, with Art.8(2) permitting proportionate interferences that are lawful and necessary in a democratic society. Any interference must be justified by pressing social need and be proportionate to the legitimate aim pursued.[395] Interference must also be '*in accordance with the law*', thus detention contrary to policy, in this case the EIG, will violate Art.8(2).[396]

The state must allow individuals to lead a normal family life,[397] while considering that the best interests of children are paramount.[398] Private life includes, *inter alia*, the individual's physical and moral integrity,[399] including mental health.[400] Thus, in *R (D) v SSHD,*[401] where the detainee received some mental healthcare but of an inadequate standard, this did not meet the Art.3 threshold, but nevertheless breached Art.8.

Detention constitutes an interference with private life, however, as the ECHR does not guarantee aliens a right to enter or remain in another state,[402] immigration control is a legitimate purpose under Art.8.[403] However the Court has stressed that in pursuing this purpose, states must comply with international obligations.[404] The Court therefore recognises the tension between immigration control and human rights, but, unlike its Art.5(1)(f) approach, it conducts a proportionality assessment, with sovereign border control interests one of many relevant factors.

Thus, Art.8 may protect vulnerable detainees whose severity of treatment does not meet the Art.3 threshold, however the ability of the state to

---

393 *R(EH) v SSHD* [2012] EWHC 2569 (Admin)

394 *Ibid.*

395 *Amrollahi v Denmark*, (2002) 22 EHHR 585 [33]

396 *Elci and Others v Turkey*, nos.23145/93/25091/94 (13 Nov.2003) [697]; *R(EH)* [220]

397 *Marckx v Belgium* 25 Series A no.31 (13 Jun.1979)

398 *Popov* [109]

399 *Bensaid v UK* [2001] 33 EHRR 10

400 *Ibid.* [46]

401 [2012] EWHC 2501 (Admin)

402 *Moustaquim v Belgium* Series A no.193 (18 Feb.1991) [43]

403 *Mitunga* [81]; *Popov* [106]

404 *Mitunga* [81]

justify interferences under Art.8(2) may still make it difficult for detainees to demonstrate a breach.[405]

UN System

Art.9 ICCPR requires the detention conditions to relate to its purpose. Thus, where immigration detainees are held in prisons, as in the UK, this may be arbitrary under Art.9.[406] Detention conditions may also engage Art.7 ICCPR. This provision is complimented by Art.10(1) ICCPR,[407] requiring the humane and dignified treatment of detainees. Art.10 recognises detainees' inherent vulnerability,[408] and requires that they are not subjected to hardship other than deprivation of liberty.[409] The HRC considers that '*treating all persons deprived of their liberty with humanity and ...respect for their dignity is a fundamental and universally applicable rule*' which must be applied without discrimination, including on grounds of race or national origin.[410]

Art.7 entails a positive duty on the state to protect detainees against torture, inhuman or degrading treatment.[411] In *C v Australia*, the author's continued detention, despite the state being aware of his mental health condition and deterioration, violated Art.7.[412] The state must also protect detainees from self-harm and suicide under Art.6 ICCPR (right to life).

Art.10 requires a lower threshold of severity in treatment than Art.7. The assessment of this threshold depends on the circumstances, such as the nature of treatment, its duration, physical or mental effects and the characteristics of the victim.[413] Lack of healthcare in detention causing significant harm may violate Art.10.[414]

In *F.J. v Australia*, the HRC considered that even where healthcare and mental support services were provided to detainees (as argued by the state party but contested by the author), this did not escape the negative impact of prolonged detention on their mental health.[415] This was another

---

405 *R(D)* [188]
406 GC.35 [18],[21]
407 HRC '*General Comment No.21: Article 10 (Humane treatment of persons deprived of their liberty)* 1992 HRI/GEN/1/Rev.9(Vol. I) [3] (Hereinafter, GC.21)
408 *Ibid.*
409 *Abdullayev v Turkmenistan* Communication no.2218/2012 (3 Sep.2012)
410 GC.21 [4]
411 HRC '*General Comment no.20: Prohibition of torture or other cruel, inhuman or degrading treatment or punishment'(1992)* A/44/40 [8]
412 [8.4]
413 *Brough v Australia* Communication no.1184/2003 (17 Mar.2006)
414 *Simpson v Jamaica* Communication no.695/1996 (19 Mar.1996)
415 *F.J* [10.6]

one of the factors that led to a violation of Art.7. The HRC considered it unnecessary to examine the communication under the lower threshold of Art.10(1).

The prohibition on torture, inhuman and degrading treatment is also contained in several other IHRL instruments, most notably UNCAT, which requires states to take effective legislative, administrative, judicial or other measures to prevent acts of torture[416] or cruel, inhuman or degrading treatment.[417] Art.11 requires detainees to be treated with a view to preventing torture. The CAT has consistently criticised the detention of children, torture survivors, trafficking victims and persons with serious mental disability in the UK, recommending an independent review of the R35 process, and the reversal of the EIG policy on mental illness.[418] In its most recent concluding observations on the UK, the CAT stated that it remains *'very concerned'* by reports that victims of torture are routinely detained for immigration purposes and that the Adults at Risk Policy and R35 process are *'largely ineffective at identifying victims of torture and have not resulted in the release from detention of the vast majority of those people who are at risk of suffering serious harm as a consequence of detention.'*[419]

The HRC requires that the detention of migrants must account for the potential impacts on physical or mental health. [420]Poor healthcare in detention also engages the right to health guaranteed in Art.12 International Covenant on Economic, Social and Cultural Rights (ICESCR).[421] States must guarantee equal access to healthcare for *'...prisoners or detainees, minorities, asylum seekers and illegal immigrants,'*[422]which includes reproductive healthcare.[423] Furthermore, the Committee on Economic Social and Cultural Rights (CESCR) has expressed concern over the *'...lack of adequate mental health care provided to persons in detention'* in the UK.[424] These obligations have done little to improve healthcare in detention, however. One reason for this may be that ESCR have traditionally

416 Art.2 UNCAT

417 *Ibid.*Art.16

418 CAT 'Concluding observations on the fifth periodic report of the United Kingdom of Great Britain and Northern Ireland' 24 June 2013 CAT/C/GBR/CO/5 [30]

419 CAT 2019 [54]

420 *Shafiq* v *Australia* Communication no.1324/2004 (31 Oct.2006) [7.3]; *C* [8.2]-[8.4]

421 1966 993 UNTS 3

422 CESCR *'General Comment no.14: Right to the Highest Attainable Standard of Health'*(2000) E/C.12/2000/4 [34]

423 CESCR *'General Comment no.22: Right to Sexual and Reproductive Health'*(2016) E/C.12/GC/22 [31]

424 CESCR *Conc.obs* [57]

been viewed as 'non-justiciable'; the UK is yet to ratify the Optional Protocol to the ICESCR that would enable individuals to complain directly to the CESCR.

In respect of the gendered harms suffered by detainees, the Convention on the Elimination of All Forms of Discrimination Against Women (CEDAW) requires states to eliminate gender discrimination by public authorities and other persons and enterprises.[425] Pursuant to Art.12 (right to health), CtEDAW highlights the special needs of pregnant women and nursing mothers, who it recommends '*as a general rule...should not be detained.*'[426]

CtEDAW emphasises the specific needs of '*...victims of sexual abuse and exploitation, of trauma and torture or ill-treatment and of other particularly vulnerable groups of women'*, recommending that all staff working with women detainees receive gender-sensitive training and that the use of female guards should be promoted.[427] Respect for women prisoners' privacy and dignity must be a high priority for prison staff.[428]

The UK's failure to address gendered vulnerabilities in detention, including maternal healthcare, trauma, lack of female staff, disrespect for privacy, and allegations of abuse by detention staff, may constitute discrimination under CEDAW.

States are also obligated to combat GBV, a form of discrimination,[429] including the acts or omissions of private bodies providing public services.[430] States must exercise due diligence in preventing, protecting from, investigating and compensating gender-based violence, as contained in other instruments, including the Council of Europe Convention on preventing and combating violence against women and domestic violence.[431]Despite this, repeated allegations of abuse and inappropriate behaviour by detention staff suggest that the UK is not exercising requisite due diligence in protecting detainees from GBV.

The detention of potential trafficking victims also questions the UK's compliance with obligations to support trafficking victims under Art.6

[425] Art.2(d)-(e)

[426] CtEDAW *'General recommendation No.32: gender-related dimensions of refugee status, asylum, nationality and statelessness of women'*(2014) CEDAW/C/GC/32 [49]

[427] *Ibid.*

[428] CtEDAW, *Abramova v Belarus,* Communication no.23/2009 (27 Sep. 2011) [7.7]

[429] CtEDAW *'General Recommendation no.19: violence against women'* (1992) *A/47/38* [8]

[430] CtEDAW *'Draft General Recommendation No.19 (1992): accelerating elimination of gender-based violence against women'* (2016) [13(a)]

[431] Council of Europe, 2014, CETS no.210

UN Protocol to Prevent, Suppress and Punish Trafficking in Persons, especially Women and Children 2000[432] and other regional instruments.

The UN Convention on the Rights of the Child (CRC)[433] permits the detention of children only as a last resort,[434] in age-appropriate conditions[435] and in the child's best interests,[436] The UN Committee on the Rights of the Child (CtRC) recommends that unaccompanied children should not be detained, and that detention of children cannot be justified by immigration status.[437] The HRC,[438] CtEDAW[439] and ECtHR[440] have also endorsed these principles. 117 children in detention is not exceptional as envisaged by the CRC, and is highly problematic given a child's inherent vulnerability. The closure of Cedars also calls into question whether future detention conditions will be age-appropriate.

Art.14 UN Convention on the Rights of Persons with Disabilities (CRPD)[441] requires detention to preserve the dignity of persons with disabilities, and guarantee their full participation in daily life.[442] The treatment of detainees with disabilities in Harmondsworth and the Verne appears to circumvent these obligations. Treatment '*bordering on the inhumane*' may constitute inhuman or degrading treatment under Art.15(2) CRPD and other instruments, as well as Art.17 CRPD which guarantees the right to respect for physical and mental integrity of individuals with disabilities.

The Yogyakarta Principles state that detention of persons should not further marginalise or subject detainees to ill-treatment on grounds of sexual orientation or gender identity, and that protection measures should not unduly restrict their rights.[443] The UNHCR detention guidelines at guideline 9.7 emphasise the obligation of states to take measures to avoid

---

432 UNGA, 2000, A/Res/55/383 40 ILM 335

433 1989, 1577 UNTS 3

434 *Ibid.*Art.37(b)

435 *Ibid.*Art.37(c)

436 Art.3 CRC

437 CtRC '*General Comment no.6: Treatment of Unaccompanied and Separated Children Outside their Country of Origin*'(2005) CRC/GC/2005/61[61]-[63]

438 *D. and E.* v *Australia* Communication no.1050/2002 (9 Aug.2006) [7.2]

439 CtEDAW GR.32 [49]

440 *Mitunga* [81]

441 2006, 2515 UNTS 3

442 Committee on the Rights of Persons with Disabilities, '*Guidelines on Article 14 of the Convention on the Rights of Persons with Disabilities*'(2015) 14th sess. [17]-[18]

443 Principle 9, Principles on the application of international human rights law in relation to sexual orientation and gender identity, (International Commission of Jurists, 2007)

exposing detainees to risk of violence, ill-treatment or physical, mental or sexual abuse on grounds of sexual orientation or gender identity, as well as ensuring that they have access to appropriate medical care and counselling.[444] The guidelines also provide that detention staff should be adequately trained regarding principles of non-discrimination, sexual orientation and gender identity.[445] In relation to the segregation of LGBTQI+ detainees, where their security cannot be guaranteed in detention, the guidelines are clear that solitary confinement is not an appropriate way to protect such persons and that release or referral to alternatives to detention should instead be sought.[446] The failure to protect LGBTQI+ detainees from abuse and use of segregation to protect them goes against these principles.

Conclusions

As opined by the High Court in June 2019, a detention centre, with its population of vulnerable persons, is a place where erosion of the rule of law may be thought to be both particularly likely and because of that, particularly dangerous.[447] It is for this reason that measures required to be taken by the state to protect vulnerable detainees must be meaningful and robust.

This chapter in particular highlights serious concerns about the effect of the privatisation of the immigration detention system more generally, and raises questions of the compatibility of private profit-making with maintaining a safe environment that prioritises the welfare of detainees.

IHRL has provided vulnerable detainees a degree of protection, particularly through invocation of ECHR jurisprudence, and, less so, UN conventions, in the domestic courts. Recent court challenges have also fed into the political conversation about the detention of vulnerable people, including the Shaw reviews and Adults at Risk policy, which, while not without flaws, is certainly a step forward.

However, under IHRL, the threshold of severity, as well the barriers to justice discussed in Ch.3, required to find a violation against, and a remedy for, vulnerable detainees can be prohibitive. In the UK, it has been

---

[444] Guideline 9.7, UNHCR '*Guidelines on the Applicable Criteria and Standards Relating to the Detention of Asylum-seekers and Alternatives to Detention*'(2012) at: http://www.unhcr.org/505b10ee9.pdf

[445] *Ibid.*

[446] Guideline 9.7, UNHCR '*Guidelines on the Applicable Criteria and Standards Relating to the Detention of Asylum-seekers and Alternatives to Detention*'(2012) at: http://www.unhcr.org/505b10ee9.pdf

[447] *MA & BB v Secretary of State for the Home Department* [2019] EWHC 1523 (Admin) [69(iii)]

highlighted that the detention of highly vulnerable persons often falls below the standards set by IHRL in many respects. Yet, so far, IHRL has only constrained harmful practices in the most severe of cases.

Conclusion

This paper has sought to demonstrate that immigration detention in the UK regularly undermines the principles of the rule of law, non-discrimination and respect for dignity that underpin IHRL. The equal humanity of non-nationals is denied through a practice of political subjugation and 'othering' that locks up individuals unnecessarily, indefinitely, without charge and often at the height of vulnerability.

In March 2019, the House of Commons Home Affairs Committee published its inquiry into immigration detention, concluding that the Home Office had a *'shockingly cavalier'* attitude towards immigration detention, had *'overseen serious failings in almost every area of the immigration detention process'* and that systemic safeguarding and case-working failures have led to people being wrongfully detained, held in immigration when they are vulnerable and detained unnecessarily for too long.[448]

Detention continues despite its inefficacy in achieving its stated objectives, its high human and financial cost and availability of less harmful alternatives. Such treatment would be almost unthinkable against citizens, and represents a particularly violent expression of the UK's unrelenting objective to create a *'hostile environment'* for immigrants.

One may consider that the IHRL system, with its proclamations of universality and equality, would be well-positioned to fairly balance sovereign interests of border control and the human rights of detainees. Yet, IHRL has provided limited protection, representing *'...an unusually clear failure of the international human rights system as a tool of legal and political change.'*[449]

The issues explored in these sections are inextricably interlinked. Detention is often prolonged by ineffective remedies and lack of access to justice; prolonged detention in particular impacts mental health and exacerbates vulnerabilities, which can then impede access to justice. The privatisation of detention has been extremely damaging, including abuse

[448] Home Affairs Committee *'Cavalier' Home Office failing in its responsibility for immigration detention'* (2019) at: https://www.parliament.uk/business/committees/committees-a-z/commons-select/home-affairs-committee/news-parliament-2017/immigration-detention-report-published-17-19/

[449] Wilsher, p.116

with impunity, harmful cost-cutting measures and profit incentives to fill beds in IRCs.[450]

Section Two demonstrated that the ECtHR interprets migrants' right to liberty as dependent on state authorisation.[451] The ECtHR allows states to detain non-nationals indefinitely, unnecessarily and, as discussed in Section Three, without equal procedural safeguards. Nowhere is this considered discriminatory. Rather, the unequal treatment of migrants is considered a *'necessary adjunct'* to sovereign power.[452] This discretion dilutes the right to equality and non-discrimination, contained in several IHRL instruments,[453] for 'unauthorised' non-nationals.[454] The HRC's interpretation of arbitrary detention is more faithful to IHRL principles, yet maintains the possibility of indefinite detention without judicial authorisation. Furthermore, it suffers from the weak enforcement mechanisms that plague the IHRL system as a whole. It is problematic that the ECtHR is the most deferential to state objectives, when its enforcement mechanisms afford it the greatest potential to alter UK practice.

Detaining highly vulnerable persons, discussed in Section Four, is removed from moral notions of humanity and has constituted inhuman and degrading treatment. Here, IHRL, particularly as invoked in the domestic courts, has protected vulnerable detainees, albeit in extreme cases. UN treaty bodies have urged the UK to respect detainees' fundamental rights, yet UK practice has remained largely immune to these criticisms.[455] The weak enforceability of IHRL has been visible throughout this discussion, and has been discussed at length elsewhere.[456]

None of the IHRL bodies discussed, with the exception of the WGAD, considers immigration detention to be problematic in principle. This stems from the assumption that immigration detention is a necessary corollary of sovereign territoriality. Detention is legitimised through the political 'othering' of irregular migrants, who are cast outside the realms of standard rights protection. The UK government's domestic legitimacy depends on this, which is part of a grander project, underpinned by institutional racism, that seeks to assert sovereign territoriality and exclude undesirables.

This political agenda presents a monumental challenge for IHRL. As Feldman observes, '*an international tribunal which fails to take account*

[450] Bacon, p.25

[451] Bryan & Langford, p.217

[452] *Saadi*

[453] e.g Art.14 ECHR; Art.2(1), Art.26 ICCPR

[454] Cornelisse, p.177

[455] Wilsher, p.170

[456] e.g Davies, M '*Rhetorical Inaction? Compliance and the Human Rights Council of the United Nations*'(2010) Alternatives 35 449–468

of political and legal reality within a State puts its own effectiveness and authority at risk.'[457] This is particularly true for the ECtHR, which must balance pragmatism against over-stretching its political legitimacy. This is underpinned by the principle of state sovereignty as a foundation of international law, which loses its effect where states are unwilling to comply with it.[458] While the UK's detention policies have been limited by IHRL to an extent, it has more often reached its own balance between migrants' rights and its immigration objectives.[459]

IHRL fails to challenge the statist assumption, or question whether borders and territoriality, which are inherently violent and discriminatory, are compatible with its universal aspirations of equality. The designation of nationality, based upon *'imagined lines on the surface of the earth,'*[460] affords some sections of humanity wealth, mobility and opportunity, confining others to immobility, inopportunity and the detention centre. As Dembour notes, the injustice of this system of exclusion and privilege has inspired grassroots 'open-border' movements, on the premise that all human beings are equal. This is the very premise that the international human rights system was supposedly founded upon. Dembour emphasises that the global system of nationality and citizenship is a social construction, and thus may, one day, be considered *'one of the greatest abominations of our time'*, on par with, for example, slavery.[461] The question of how to re-formulate this system to one that truly reflects values of equality and humanity, while overcoming claims to power and privilege, is one that goes beyond the scope of this discussion, and perhaps beyond IHRL, which remains relatively state-centric. It is nevertheless important to question whether claims to territorial sovereignty, justifying immigration detention, are inevitable and innocent.[462]

IHRL will have greater capacity to protect immigration detainees in the UK when these ideas are challenged. This begins to appear in ECtHR judgments concerning extreme vulnerability, where the Court holds that the prerogative to control borders cannot absolve states of their obligations to prevent inhuman treatment.[463] Yet, IHRL must do more, even accounting for considerations of legitimacy, to promote a system that truly considers humans of equal worth – migrant or citizen.[464]

---

457 Feldman, D '*Sovereignties in Strasbourg*' in Rawlings, R, Leyland, P and Young, A (eds) '*Sovereignty and the Law: Domestic, European and International Perspectives*'(2013) Oxford: Oxford University Press p.223

458 *Ibid.*p.218

459 Wilsher, p.321

460 Cornelisse, p.137

461 Dembour, p.30

462 Cornelisse, p.310

463 *Mitunga; M.S.S*

464 Dembour, p.31

The failure of IHRL to protect immigration detainees, beyond the most extreme cases, begs the question of who has human rights, and points to a *de facto* reality that rights are conditional upon citizenship. While claims of territorial sovereignty remain unchallenged and 'othering' of migrants continues, IHRL will struggle to constrain – let alone abolish - immigration detention.

List of Abbreviations

BID. Bail for Immigration Detainees
BOP. United Nations Body of Principles for the Protection of All Persons under Any Form of Detention or Imprisonment
CAT. United Nations Committee Against Torture
CEDAW. Convention on the Elimination of All Forms of Discrimination Against Women 1979
CESCR. Committee on Economic, Social and Cultural Rights
CRC. United Nations Convention on the Rights of the Child 1989
CRPD. United Nations Convention on the Rights of Persons with Disabilities 2006.
CtEDAW. Committee on the Elimination of Discrimination Against Women
CtRC. United Nations Committee on the Rights of the Child
CtRPD. United Nations Committee on the Rights of Persons with Disabilities
DCR. Detention Centre Rules
DFT. Detained Fast Track
DSO. Detention Services Order
ECC. Executive Committee Conclusion
ECHR. European Convention on Human Rights 1950
ECtHR. European Court of Human Rights
EIG. Enforcement Instructions and Guidance
EU. European Union
FNO. Foreign-National ex-Offender
GBV. Gender-based Violence
GC. General Comment
HMIP. Her Majesty's Inspectorate of Prisons
HRC. Human Rights Committee
IA. Immigration Act
IACtHR. Inter-American Court of Human rights
ICCPR. International Covenant on Civil and Political Rights 1966
ICESCR. International Covenant on Economic, Social and Cultural Rights 1966
IHRL. International Human Rights Law
IMB. Independent Monitoring Board

IRC. Immigration Removal Centre
LASPO. Legal Aid, Sentencing and Punishment of Offenders Act 2012
LGBTI. Lesbian Gay Bisexual Transgender Intersex
MJ. Medical Justice
MPR. Monthly Progress Report
PTSD. Post Traumatic Stress Disorder
R35. Rule 35 Detention Centre Rules 2001
SRHRM. United Nations Special Rapporteur on the Human Rights of Migrants
SSHD. Secretary of State for the Home Department
UK. United Kingdom
UKIP. United Kingdom Independence Party
UN. United Nations
UNCAT. United Nations Convention on the Prohibition of Torture and Other Cruel, Inhuman and Degrading Treatment or Punishment 1984
UNGA. United Nations General Assembly
UNHCR. United Nations High Commissioner for Refugees
WGAD. Working Group on Arbitrary Detention

References

International and Regional Human Rights Law Instruments

American Convention on Human Rights (Organization of American State 'Pact of San Jose', Costa Rica, 22 November 1969)

Convention for the Protection of Human Rights and Fundamental Freedoms (European Convention on Human Rights, as amended) 1950 ETS 5

Convention Relating to the Status of Refugees (adopted 28 July 1951, entered into force 22 April 1954) 189 UNTS 137 (Refugee Convention)

Council of Europe, Council of Europe Convention on preventing and combating violence against women and domestic violence 2014 CETS No.210

Explanatory Report on Protocol No.7 ECHR ETS 117

International Covenant on Civil and Political Rights (adopted 16 December 1966, entered into force 23 March 1976) 999 UNTS 171 (ICCPR)

International Covenant on Economic, Social and Cultural Rights (adopted 16 December 1966, entered into force 23 March 1976) 993 UNTS 3

UN Convention against Torture and Other Cruel, Inhuman or Degrading Treatment or Punishment (UNCAT) 1984, 1465 UNTS 85
UN Convention on the Rights of Persons with Disabilities 2006, 2515 UNTS 3
UN Convention on the Rights of the Child 1989, 1577 UNTS 3
UNGA, UN Protocol to Prevent, Suppress and Punish Trafficking in Persons, especially Women and Children 2000 A/Res/55/383 40 ILM 335
Universal Declaration of Human Rights (adopted 10 December 1948 UNGA Res 217 A(III)

EU Law

Asylum Procedures Directive 2005/85/EC
Reception Conditions Directive 2003/9/EC
Returns Directive 2008/115/EC

UK domestic legislation

Bail Act 1976
Criminal Procedure (Scotland) Act
Detention Centre Rules 2001
Equality Act 2010
Human Rights Act 1998
Immigration Act 1971
Immigration Act 2014
Immigration Act 2016
Immigration and Asylum Act 1999
Legal Aid, Sentencing and Punishment of Offenders Act 2012
Police and Criminal Evidence Act 1984
Protection of Freedoms Act 2012

Bills

Immigration (Time Limit on Detention) Bill 2019

European Court/Commission on Human Rights Case Law

A and Others v UK (2009) 49 EHRR 29
Aerts v Belgium (2000) 29 EHRR 50
Amrollahi v Denmark, (2002) 22 EHHR 585
Amuur v France (1996) 22 EHRR 533

Arben Draga v United Kingdom Application no. 33341/13 (25 April 2017)
Aydin v Turkey [1997] ECHR 75
Bensaid v UK [2001] 33 EHRR 10
Caprino v United Kingdom Application no.6871/75 (3 Mar.1978)
Chahal v UK [1996] ECHR 54
Charahili v Turkey Application no. 46605/07 (13 Apr.2010)
Čonka v Belgium Application no.51564/99 (5 Feb.2002)
De Wilde Ooms and Versyp v Belgium (1971) 1 EHRR 373
Dougoz v Greece [2001] ECHR 213
Elci and Others v. Turkey, nos.23145/93/25091/94 (13 Nov.2003)
Hirst v UK (No 2)[2005]ECHR 681
Ireland v UK [1978] ECHR 1
J.N. v UK [2016] ECHR 434
Keenan v UK [2001] ECHR 242
Kudła v Poland [2000] ECHR 512
Louled Massoud v Malta Application no. 24340/08 (27 Jul.2010)
Lynas v Switzerland Application no.7317/75 (6.Oct.1967)
Maaouia v France [2000] ECHR 455
Marckx v Belgium 25 Series A no. 31 (13 Jun.1979)
Mikolenko v Estonia App. no. 16944/03, 5 January 2006
Moustaquim v Belgium Series A no.193 (18 Feb.1991)
Mubilanzila Mayeka and Kaniki Mitunga v Belgium Application no. 13178/03 (12 Oct.2006)
Muminov v Russia Application no. 42502/06 (11 Dec.2008)
Nasrulloyev v Russia, Application no.656/06 (11 Oct.2007)
Öcalan v Turkey [2005] ECHR 282
Popov v France Applications nos. 39472/07 and 39474/07, 19 January 2012
Pretty v UK (2002) 35 EHRR 1
Rahimi v Greece Application no. 8687/08 5 Apr.2011
R.C. v Sweden Application no.41827/07 (9 Mar.2010)
Rohde v Denmark (2005) 43 EHRR 325
Saadi v UK [2008] ECHR 80
Slimani v France (2006) 43 EHRR 49
Soering v UK [1989] 11 EHRR 439
Storck v Germany (2005) 43 EHRR 96 [74]
V.M. v UK Application no. 49734/12 1 Sep.2016
Varbanov v Bulgaria (2000) Reports 2000-X
Weeks v UK [1987] ECHR 3
Winterwerp v Netherlands [1979] ECHR 4
Yoh-Ekale Mwanje v Belgium Application no.10486/10 20 Dec.2011
Zamir v UK (1983) 5 EHRR 242

Human Rights Committee Case Law

A v Australia Communication No.560/1993 (30 April 1997)
Abdullayev v Turkmenistan Communication no.2218/2012 (3 Sep.2012)
Baban v Australia Communication No. 1014/2001 (6 Aug.2003)
Brough v Australia Communication no.1184/2003 (17 Mar.2006)
C v Australia Communication No. 900/1999 (28 Oct.2002)
D. and E. v Australia Communication no.1050/2002 (9 Aug.2006
F.J.et al v Australia Communication no. 2233/2013 (2 May-2016)
Fongum Gorji-Dinka v Cameroon Communication no. 1134/2002 (17 Mar.2005)
Gavrilin v Belarus Communication No. 1342/2005 (28 Oct.2004)
M.M.M.et al. v Australia Communication no.2136/201225 (28 Oct. 2013)
Shafiq v Australia Communication no. 1324/2004 (31 Oct.2006)
Shams et al v Australia Communication No. 1255/2004 (11 Sep.2007)
Simpson v Jamaica Communication no.695/1996 (19 Mar.1996)

Other Case Law

Committee on the Elimination of Discrimination Against Women

CtEDAW, Abramova v Belarus, Communication No. 23/2009 (27 Sep. 2011)

European Court of Justice

Case C215/03 Oulane v Minister voor Vreemdelingenzaken en Integratie [2005] ECR I 1215

Inter-American Court of Human Rights

Vélez Loor v Panama, Preliminary Objections, Merits, Reparations and Costs, Judgment (IACtHR)(23 Nov. 2010)
Advisory Opinion on Juridical Condition and Rights of the Undocumented Migrants, OC-18/03 (IACtHR) 17 September 2003

International Criminal Tribunal for the former Yugoslavia

Prosecutor v Furundzija (IT-95-17/1-T) ICTY Trial Chamber (10 Dec. 1998)

Working Group on Arbitrary Detention

WGAD, Abdi v United Kingdom of Great Britain and Northern Ireland (2007) Opinion no.45/2006, A/HRC/7/4/Add.1

UN Treaty Bodies General Recommendations, Comments and Concluding Observations

CAT '*Concluding observations on the fifth periodic report of the United Kingdom of Great Britain and Northern Ireland*' 24 June 2013 CAT/C/GBR/CO/5

CAT '*Concluding observations on the sixth periodic report of the United Kingdom of Great Britain and Northern Ireland*' 7 June 2019 CAT/C/GBR/CO/6

CESCR '*General Comment no.14 on the Right to the Highest Attainable Standard of Health*'(2000) E/C.12/2000/4

CESCR '*General Comment no.22 on the Right to Sexual and Reproductive Health*'(2016) E/C.12/GC/22

Committee on the Rights of Persons with Disabilities, '*Guidelines on Article 14 of the Convention on the Rights of Persons with Disabilities*'(2015) 14th sess.

CtEDAW '*Draft General Recommendation No. 19 (1992): accelerating elimination of gender-based violence against women*' (2016)

CtEDAW '*General recommendation No. 32 on the gender-related dimensions of refugee status, asylum, nationality and statelessness of women*'(2014) CEDAW/C/GC/32

CtEDAW '*General Recommendation no.19: violence against women*'(1992) *A/47/*

CtRC '*General Comment no.6: Treatment of Unaccompanied and Separated Children Outside their Country of Origin*'(2005) CRC/GC/2005/61

HRC '*Concluding observations on the seventh periodic report of the United Kingdom of Great Britain and Northern Ireland*' (2015) CCPR/C/GBR/CO/7

HRC '*General Comment no.15:The Position of Aliens Under the Covenant*' 27thsess(11 Apr.1986)

HRC '*General Comment no.20: Prohibition of torture or other cruel, inhuman or degrading treatment or punishment'(1992)* A/44/40

HRC '*General Comment No.21: Article 10 (Humane treatment of persons deprived of their liberty)* 1992 HRI/GEN/1/Rev.9(Vol. I)

HRC '*General Comment No.35: Article 9(Liberty and Security of Person)*' CCPR/C/GC/35

Other Soft Law and Guidelines

International Commission of Jurists, Yogyakarta Principles: Principles on the application of international human rights law in relation to sexual orientation and gender identity, 2007

UNGA Human Rights Council, '*Report of the Special Rapporteur on the human rights of migrants, Jorge Bustamante: Mission to the United Kingdom of Great Britain and Northern Ireland*' (2010) A/HRC/14/30/Add.3

UNGA Res.63/184 '*Protection of Migrants,*'(2009) 63rd sess, [9]A/RES/63/184

UNGA Res.64/166 '*Protection of Migrants*'(2010) 64th sess A/RES/64/166 [4(a)]

UNGA, Human Rights Council, '*Report of the Special Rapporteur on violence against women, its causes and consequences, Rashida Manjoo: Mission to the United Kingdom of Great Britain and Northern Ireland*' (2015) A/HRC/29/27/Add.2

UNGA, Human Rights Council, Resolution 15/16'*Human Rights of* Migrants'(2010)A/HRC/RES/15/16

UNGA, *Report of the Working Group on Arbitrary* Detention'(2010) A/HRC/13/

UNGA, United Nations Body of Principles for the Protection of All Persons under Any Form of Detention or Imprisonment, 9 December 1988, A/RES/43/173

UNGA, United Nations Rules for the Treatment of Women Prisoners and Non-Custodial Measures for Women Offenders (the Bangkok Rules) 6 October 2010, A/C.3/65/L.5

UNHCR '*Guidelines on the Applicable Criteria and Standards Relating to the Detention of Asylum-seekers and Alternatives to Detention*'(2012) at: http://www.unhcr.org/505b10ee9.pdf

UNHCR and OHCHR Global Roundtable on Alternatives to Detention of Asylum-Seekers, Refugees, Migrants and Stateless Persons Geneva, 11-12 (2011) at:http://www.unhcr.org/536a00576.pdf

UNHCR Executive Committee Conclusion (1968) No.44 (XXXVII)

UK Domestic Case Law

AMM (A Child) v SSHD [2012] EWHC 2567 (QB)

Cadder v HM Advocate [2010] UKSC 43

Detention Action v SSHD [2014] EWHC 2245 (Admin)

Farquharson (removal- proof of conduct) [2013] UKUT 146 (IAC)

Gedi v SSHD [2016] EWCA Civ 409

MA & BB v Secretary of State for the Home Department [2019] EWHC 1523 (Admin)

Medical Justice & Ors v SSHD [2017] EWHC 2461 (Admin) [154]
R (BA) v SSHD [2011] EWHC 2748 (Admin)
R (D) v SSHD [2012] EWHC 2501 (Admin)
R (Davies) v Secretary of State for the Home Department (SSHD) [2010] EWHC 2656 (Admin)
R (EH) v SSHD [2012] EWHC 2569 (Admin)
R (Giwa) v SSHD [2013] EWHC 3189 (Admin)
R (Hardial Singh) v Governor of Durham Prison [1983] EWHC 1 (QB)
R (Iqbal) v SSHD [2015] EWCA Civ 838
R (Joint Council for the Welfare of Immigrants) v Secretary of State for the Home Department [2019] EWHC 452 (Admin)
R (on the application of Nouazli) v SSHD [2016] UKSC
R (VC) v SSHD [2018] EWCA Civ 57
R (Xue) v SSHD [2015] EWHC 825 (Admin)
Walumba Lumba & Kadian Mighty v SSHD [2011] UKSC 12

Books

Agamben, G 'Homo Sacer: Sovereign Power and Bare Life'(1998) Stanford University Press
Agamben, G 'State of Exception'(2005) University of Chicago Press
Ashford, M '*Detained Without Trial: A Survery of Immigration Act Detention*'(1993) Joint
Council for the Welfare of Immigrants
Bantekas, I and Oette, L '*International Human Rights Law and Practice*' (2016) 2 edn. Cambridge: Cambridge University Press
Blake, N and Husain, R '*Immigration, Asylum & Human Rights*' (2003) Oxford: Oxford University Press
Bosworth, M 'Inside Immigration Detention'(2014) Oxford: Oxford University Press
Bosworth, M and Kellezi, B '*Citizenship and Belonging in a Women's Immigration Detention Centre*' (2013) In C. Philips and C. Webster (Eds.). (2014). New Directions in Race and Ethnicity. Abingdon: Routledge; Criminal Justice, Borders and Citizenship Research Paper No. 2448450
Bosworth, M, Parmar, A and Vázquez, Y '*Race, Criminal Justice, and Migration Control: Enforcing the Boundaries of Belonging*' (2018) Oxford University Press
Conte, A and Burchill '*Defining civil and political rights the jurisprudence of the United Nations Human Rights Committee*' (2009) 2edn. Routledge
Cornelisse, G '*Immigration Detention and Human Rights: Rethinking Territorial*
Sovereignty' (2010) Leiden: Martinus Nijhoff

Costello, C *'The Human Rights of Migrants in European Law'*(2016) Oxford: Oxford University

d'Orey, S *'Immigration prisoners:a forgotten minority'*(1984) London: Runnymede Trust

Dembour, M-B *'When Humans Become Migrants: Study of the European Court of Human Rights with an Inter-American Counterpoint'* (2015) Oxford: Oxford University Press

Denholm, G and Dunlop, R *'Detention Under the Immigration Acts: Law and Practice'* (2015) Oxford University Press, Oxford

Feldman, D *'Sovereignties in Strasbourg'* in Rawlings, R, Leyland, P and Young, A (eds) *'Sovereignty and the Law: Domestic, European and International Perspectives'*(2013) Oxford: Oxford University Press

Grimm, D *'Sovereignty: The Origin and Future of a Political and Legal Concept'* (2015) Columbia University Press

Harris, DJ, O'Boyle, M, Bates, E and Buckley, C *'Law of the European Convention on Human Rights'* (2009) 2 edn. Oxford: Oxford Univeristy Press

Higgins, R *'Problems and Process: International Law and How We Use It'* 1995 Oxford University Press

Hughes, J and Liebaut, F (eds) *'Detention of Asylum Seekers in Europe: Analysis and* Perspectives'(1998) Martinus Nijhoff

Kapur, I 'The Postcolonial Politics of Development'(2008) Routledge

Mutua, M, 'Human Rights: A Political and Cultural Critique'(2002) Philadelphia: University of Pennsylvania Press

Said, E 'Orientalism' (1985) London: Peregrine p.300

Wilsher D 'Immigration Detention: Law, History, Politics'(2012) Cambridge: Cambridge University Press

Wong, T *'Rights, Deportation, and Detention in the Age of Immigration Control'*(2015) Stanford: Stanford University Press

UK Government/Parliamentary Publications

All Party Parliamentary Group on Refugees & All Party Parliamentary Group on Migration 'T*he Report of the Inquiry into the Use of Immigration Detention in the United Kingdom'*(2015)

Clements, *'Bail Guidance for Judges Presiding Over Immigration and Asylum Hearings'* June 2012 First-Tier Tribunal (Immigration and Asylum Chamber) at: https://www.judiciary.gov.uk/wp-content/uploads/2014/07/bail-guidance-immigration-judges.pdf

Gower, M *'Immigration Detention in the UK: An Overview'*(2015) House of Commons Briefing Paper Number 7294 at: http://researchbriefings.files.parliament.uk/documents/CBP-7294/CBP-7294.pdf

Home Affairs Select Committee Q4 2015, HC 22 at https://publications.parliament.uk/pa/cm201617/cmselect/cmhaff/22/22.pdf

House of Commons Home Affairs Committee *'Immigration Detention - Fourteenth Report of Session 2017-2019'* (2019) at: https://publications.parliament.uk/pa/cm201719/cmselect/cmhaff/913/913.pdf

House of Commons, House of Lords, Joint Committee on Human Rights *'Immigration detention – Sixteenth Report of Session 2017-2019'* (2019) at: https://publications.parliament.uk/pa/jt201719/jtselect/jtrights/1484/1484.pdf

Shaw, S *'Review into the Welfare in Detention of Vulnerable Persons: A report to the Home Office by Stephen Shaw'* January 2016 p.22 at https://www.gov.uk/government/uploads/system/uploads/attachment_data/file/490782/52532_Shaw_Review_Accessible.pdf

Shaw, S, *'Assessment of government progress in implementing the report on the welfare in detention of vulnerable persons: A follow-up report to the Home Office by Stephen Shaw'* (2018) p.viii available at: https://assets.publishing.service.gov.uk/government/uploads/system/uploads/attachment_data/file/728376/Shaw_report_2018_Final_web_accessible.pdf

UK Home Office *'Adults at Risk in Detention'* (2019) at: https://assets.publishing.service.gov.uk/government/uploads/system/uploads/attachment_data/file/784634/adults-at-risk-policy-v5.0ext.pdf

UK Home Office, *'Chapter 55a Detention of pregnant women'* (2018) at: https://assets.publishing.service.gov.uk/government/uploads/system/uploads/attachment_data/file/653012/Chapter_55a_Detention_of_pregnant_women_v1.pdf

UK Home Office, 'Detention Services Order 02/2017 Removal from Association (Detention Centre Rule 40) and Temporary Confinement (Detention Centre Rule 42)' (2017) at: https://assets.publishing.service.gov.uk/government/uploads/system/uploads/attachment_data/file/630008/DSO_02_2017_-_Rule_40_and_42.pdf

UK Home Office *'Section 55: Enforcement Instructions and Guidance'* para.55.1.1 at: https://www.gov.uk/government/uploads/system/uploads/attachment_data/file/537065/Ch55_detention_and_temporary_release_v20.pdf

UK Home Office *'Detained Fast Track Processes'* at: https://www.gov.uk/government/uploads/system/uploads/attachment_data/file/370322/Detained_Fast_Track_Processes_v6_0.pdf

UK Home Office 'Home Secretary statement on immigration detention and Shaw report' (2018) at: https://www.gov.uk/government/speeches/home-secretary-statement-on-immigration-detention-and-shaw-report

UK Home Office *'Written Statement made by: The Minister of State for Immigration (James Brokenshire)'* July 2015 at: http://www.parliament.uk/documents/commons-vote-office/July%202015/2%20July/6-Home-Asylum.pdf

UK Home Office, *'Enforcement Instructions and Guidance'* Section 55, para.55.1.3 at: https://www.gov.uk/government/uploads/system/uploads/attachment_data/file/537065/Ch55_detention_and_temporary_release_v20.pdf

UK Home Office, *'Immigration Act 2016: Guidance on adults at risk in immigration detention'*(2016) at: https://www.gov.uk/government/uploads/system/uploads/attachment_data/file/547519/Adults_at_Risk_August_2016.pdf

UK Home Office 'National Statistics: How many people are detained or returned?' (2018) at: https://www.gov.uk/government/publications/immigration-statistics-year-ending-march-2018/how-many-people-are-detained-or-returned

UK Home Office, *'New commitments to tackling vulnerability in immigration detention announced'* (2018) at: https://www.gov.uk/government/news/new-commitments-to-tackling-vulnerability-in-immigration-detention-announced

UK Ministry of Justice 'Post-Implementation Review of Part 1 of the Legal Aid, Sentencing and Punishment of Offenders Act 2012 (LASPO)' (2019) at: https://assets.publishing.service.gov.uk/government/uploads/system/uploads/attachment_data/file/777038/post-implementation-review-of-part-1-of-laspo.pdf

Hansard

HL Deb 10 May 2016 vol 771 c1668

Journal Articles

Bacon, C *'The Evolution of Immigration Detention in the UK: the Involvement of Private Prison Companies'* (2005) RSC Working Paper No.27

Baldaccini, A *'The European Directive on Returns: Principles and Protests'*(2010) 28(4) Refugee Survey Quarterly 114-38

Bhui, H S, *'The place of 'race' in understanding immigration control and the detention of foreign nationals'* (2016) Criminology & Criminal Justice 2016, Vol.16(3) 267-285

Bryan, I Langford, P *'The Lawful Detention of Unauthorised Aliens under the European System for the Protection of Human Rights'*(2011) Nordic Journal of International Law 80 193–218

Charlesworth, H, Chinkin, C, Wright, S *'Feminist Approaches to International Law'*(1991) American Journal of International Law, Vol. 85(4) 613-645

Coffey, GJ, Kaplan, I, Sampson, RC, Montagna Tucci, M *'The meaning and mental health consequences of long-term immigration detention for people seeking asylum'* (2010) Social Science & Medicine 70 2070-2079

Cornelisse, G *'Human Rights for Immigration Detainees in Strasbourg: Limited Sovereignty or a Limited Discourse?'* (2004) European Journal of Migration and Law 6:93-110

Costello, C *'Human Rights and the Elusive Universal Subject: Immigration Detention Under International Human Rights and EU Law'* (2012) Indiana Journal of Global Legal Studies, Vol. 19(1) 257-303

Davies, M *'Rhetorical Inaction? Compliance and the Human Rights Council of the United Nations'*(2010) Alternatives 35 449–468

Flynn, M *'Who Must be Detained? Proportionality as a Tool for Critiquing Immigration Detention Policy'*(2012) Refugee Survey Quarterly, pp.1–29 p.11

Grant, S *'Immigration Detention: Some Issues of Inequality'*(2011) The Equal Rights Review, Vol.7 69-82

Johnston, C *'Indefinite Immigration Detention: Can it Be Justified?'*(2009) Journal of Immigration, Asylum and Nationality Law, 23(4) 351-364

Malloch, M and Stanley, E *'The Detention of Asylum-Seekers in the UK: Representing Risk, Managing the Dangerous'*(2005) Punishment and Society 1462-4745; Vol 7(1): 53–71

Marong, C *'Protecting the Public? Challenging the Indefinite Preventative Detention of Non-Citizens'* (2014) UCL Journal of Law and Jurisprudence Vol.3(1) 115-143

Money, J *'Human Rights Norms and Immigration Control'*(1998) 3 UCLA J. Int'l L. & Foreign Aff.497

Rajaram, PK and Grundy-Warr,C *'The Irregular Migrant as Homo Sacer:Migration and Detention in Australia, Malaysia, and Thailand'*(2004) International Migration Vol.42(1) 33-64

Sampson, R and Mitchell, G *'Global Trends in Immigration Detention and Alternatives to Detention Practical, Political and Symbolic Rationales'* (2013) *JMHS Vol.(1)3 97-121*

Schuster, L *'A Sledgehammer to Crack a Nut: Deportation, Detention and Dispersal in Europe'* (2005) Social Policy & Administration, Vol. 39(6) 606-621

Tyler, I *'Welcome to Britain: The cultural politics of Asylum'*(2006) *European Journal of Cultural Studies* Vol.9(2) 185-202

Welch, M and Schuster, L *'Detention of asylum seekers in the UK and USA: Deciphering noisy and quiet constructions'*(2005) Punishment & Society 1462-4745; Vol 7(4): 397–417

Wolton, S *'Immigration Policy and the "Crisis of British Values"'* (2006) Citizenship Studies Vol.10(4) 453-467

York, S *'The end of legal aid in immigration - a barrier to access to justice for migrants and a decline in the rule of law'*(2013) J.I.A.N.L. 27(2),106-138

Non-Governmental Organisation Publications

Amnesty International, *'A Matter of Routine: Immigration Detention in the UK'* (2017) at: https://www.libertyhumanrights.org.uk/sites/default/files/A%20Matter%20Of%20Routine%20ADVANCE%20-COPY.pdf

Association of Visitors to Immigration Detainees, *'Immigration Detention Statistics for 2017'* (2018) http://www.aviddetention.org.uk/news-events/news/immigration-detention-statistics-2017

Bail for Immigration Detainees *'A nice judge on a good day: immigration bail and the right to liberty'*(2010) at: http://www.biduk.org/sites/default/files/AGoodJudgeREPORT.pdf

Bail for Immigration Detainees, *'Legal advice Survey – Spring 2016'*(2016) at: http://www.biduk.org/sites/default/files/media/docs/Legal%20Advice%20Survey%20-%20Spring%202016_1.pdf

Bail for Immigration Detainees *'Liberty Deficit: Long-term detention and bail decision-making'*(2012) at: http://www.biduk.org/sites/default/files/BID%20report%20The%20Liberty%20Deficit%20December%202012_0.pdf

Bail for Immigration Detainees *'Six-monthly survey reveals lack of legal representation for immigration detainees'* (2018) at: https://www.biduk.org/posts/429-six-monthly-survey-reveals-lack-of-legal-representation-for-immigration-detainees

Bail for Immigration Detainees *'Submission to the APPG on Refugees and APPG on Migration's Parliamentary Inquiry into the Use of Immigration Detention in the UK'* (2014) at: http://www.biduk.org/sites/default/files/BID%20submission%20to%20detention%20inquiry_Access%20to%20legal%20advice%20in%20IRCs%20Sept%202014%20(2).pdf

Fordham QC, Stefanelli, JN and Eser, S *'Immigration Detention and the Rule of Law: Safeguarding Principles'*(2013) Bingham Centre for the Rule of Law at: http://www.biicl.org/files/6559_immigration_detention_and_the_rol_-_web_version.pdf

Detention Action *'Detained Lives: the real cost of indefinite immigration detention'*(2009) at: http://detentionaction.org.uk/wordpress/wp-content/uploads/2011/10/Detained-Lives-report.pdf

Detention Forum *'Rethinking 'Vulnerability' in Detention: a Crisis of Harm'*(2015) p.53 at: http://detentionforum.org.uk/wp-content/uploads/2015/07/rethinkingvulnerability_8july.pdf

Equality and Human Rights Commission *'EHRC Submission to the UN Committee Against Torture: list of issues on the UK's 5th periodic report'* (2012) at: https://www.equalityhumanrights.com/en/file/4716/download?token=bnnYklqz

Equality and Human Rights Commission *'Human Rights Review 2012: How fair is Britain?*

An assessment of how well public authorities protect human rights'(2012) at: https://www.equalityhumanrights.com/sites/default/files/hrr2012_executive_summary.pdf

Evans, M *'Rethinking legal aid: an independent strategic review'* (2018) at: https://www.gov.scot/binaries/content/documents/govscot/publications/factsheet/2018/02/rethinking-legal-aid-an-independent-strategic-review/documents/rethinking-legal-aid-independent-strategic-review-pdf/rethinking-legal-aid-independent-strategic-review-pdf/govscot:document/Rethinking%20Legal%20Aid%20-%20an%20independent%20strategic%20review.pdf

Harvey, A & Karnik, M 'Public law problems arising from the Immigration Act 2016' (2016) Immigration Law Practitioners' Association and Garden Court North Chambers at: http://www.ilpa.org.uk/data/resources/32318/16.07.14-Public-Law-Problems-arising-from-the-Immigration-Act-2016-PLP-conference-paper.pdf

International Detention Coalition *'There Are Alternatives: A handbook for preventing unnecessary immigration detention (revised edition)'*(2015) at: http://idcoalition.org/publication/there-are-alternatives-revised-edition/

Jesuit Refugee Service *'Becoming Vulnerable in Detention'* (2010) at: http://www.europarl.europa.eu/document/activities/cont/201110/20111014ATT29338/20111014ATT29338EN.pdf

Law Society of Scotland *'Inquiry into Immigration Detention'* (2018) at: https://www.lawscot.org.uk/media/361494/18-11-21-imm-inquiry-immigration-detention.pdf

Liberty, *'Liberty's response to the draft Home Office DSO on Removal from Association and Temporary Confinement'* (2016) at: https://www.liberty-human-rights.org.uk/sites/default/files/Liberty's%20Response%20to%20the%20DSO%20on%20Removal%20from%20Association%20and%20Temporary%20Confinement.pdf

Liberty, '*The case for a time limit on immigration detention has never been clearer*' (2016) at https://www.liberty-human-rights.org.uk/news/blog/case-time-limit-immigration-detention-has-never-been-clearer

Medical Justice '*A Secret Punishment: The Misuse of Segregation in Immigration Detention*'(2015) at: http://www.medicaljustice.org.uk/wpcontent/uploads/2016/05/MJ_Segregation_report_WEB_version_04_11_15-1.pdf

Medical Justice '*Biased and Unjust: The Immigration Detention Complaints Process*' (2016) http://www.medicaljustice.org.uk/wp-content/uploads/2016/03/BiasedandUnjustReport.pdf

Medical Justice '*Expecting Change: The case for ending the detention of pregnant women*'(2013) at: http://www.medicaljustice.org.uk/wp-content/uploads/2016/03/expectingchange.pdf

Medical Justice '*Healthcare in Detention: Written Evidence Submitted by Medical Justice to the Shaw Review*'(2015) p.1 at: http://www.medicaljustice.org.uk/wp-content/uploads/2016/04/althcareinDetention-SummarybyMedicalJusticeforShawReview.pdf

Medical Justice '*Outsourcing Abuse*'(2008) at: http://www.medicaljustice.org.uk/wp-content/uploads/2016/03/outsourcing-abuse.pdf

Redress, '*Austerity & Legal Aid: Impact on the vulnerable*' (2014) at: http://www.redress.org/downloads/publications/10Oct2014-austerity-and-legal-aid-conference-paper.pdf

Royal College of Psychiatrists, '*Position Statement on detention of people with mental disorders in Immigration Removal Centres*'(2015) at: http://www.rcpsych.ac.uk/pdf/Satisfactory%20Treatment%20in%20Detention%20document%20December%202015%20edit.pdf

Silverman, S and Hajela, R '*Briefing: Immigration Detention in the UK*' February 2016, Migration Observatory, University of Oxford at: http://www.migrationobservatory.ox.ac.uk/sites/files/migobs/Immigration%20Detention%20Briefing.pdf

Stonewall and UK Lesbian & Gay Immigration Group '*No Safe Refuge: Experiences of LGBT Asylum Seekers in Detention*' (2016) at: https://www.stonewall.org.uk/system/files/no_safe_refuge.pdf

Tsangarides, N '*The Second Torture: the Immigration Detention of Torture Survivors*'(2012) Medical Justice at: http://www.medicaljustice.org.uk/wp-content/uploads/2016/03/the-second-torture-full-version.pdf

UNHCR '*Inquiry into the use of Immigration Detention: Written Evidence to the Parliamentary Joint* Committee'(2014) at: http://www.refworld.org/docid/54f590ab4.html

Women for Refugee Women '*I Am Human: Refugee Women's Experiences of Detention in the UK*'(2015) at: http://www.refugeewomen.-

co.uk/2016/wp-content/uploads/2016/02/WRW_IamHuman_report-for-web.pdf

Reports of Independent Inspectorates

HM Inspectorate of Prisons (HMIP) and Independent Chief Inspector of Borders and Immigration, '*The effectiveness and impact of immigration detention casework*' (2012) at: http://icinspector.independent.gov.uk/wp-content/uploads/2012/12/Immigration-detention-casework-2012-FINAL.pdf

HMIP '*Annual Report 2015-2016*' (2016) at: https://www.gov.uk/government/uploads/system/uploads/attachment_data/file/538854/hmip-annual-report.pdf

HMIP '*Harmondsworth immigration removal centre – persistent failings in safety and respect*' (2018) at: https://www.justiceinspectorates.gov.uk/hmiprisons/media/press-releases/2018/03/harmondsworth-immigration-removal-centre-persistent-failings-in-safety-and-respect/

HMIP '*Report on an Unannounced Inspection of Campsfield House Immigration Removal Centre*'(2014) at: https://www.justiceinspectorates.gov.uk/hmiprisons/wp-content/uploads/sites/4/2015/02/Campsfield-House-web-2014.pdf

HMIP '*Report on an Unannounced Inspection of Cedars pre-departure accommodation and overseas family escort Immigration Removal Centre*'(2014) at: https://www.justice.gov.uk/about/hmi-prisons/?a=101086

HMIP '*Report on an Unannounced inspection of Colnbrook Immigration Removal Centre*' 2016 at https://www.justiceinspectorates.gov.uk/hmiprisons/wp-content/uploads/sites/4/2016/07/Colnbrook-Web-2016.pdf

HMIP '*Report on an Unannounced Inspection of Dungavel House Immigration Removal Centre*'(2015) at: https://www.justiceinspectorates.gov.uk/hmiprisons/wp-content/uploads/sites/4/2015/07/Dungavel-web-2015.pdf

HMIP '*Report on an Unannounced Inspection of Harmondsworth Immigration Removal Centre*' (2013) at: http://www.migrantsrights.org.uk/files/news/14.01.16-HMIP-Harmondsworth-IRC-5-16-August-2013.pdf

HMIP '*Report on an Unannounced Inspection of Heathrow Immigration Removal Centre, Harvard Site*'(2015) at: https://www.justiceinspectorates.gov.uk/hmiprisons/wp-content/uploads/sites/4/2016/02/Harmondsworth-web-2015.pdf

HMIP '*Report on an Unannounced Inspection of The Verne Immigration Removal Centre*'(2015) at: https://www.justiceinspectorates.gov.uk/

hmiprisons/wp-content/uploads/sites/4/2015/08/The-Verne-web-2015.pdf

HMIP '*Report on an Unannounced Inspection of Tinsley House Immigration Removal Centre*'(2014) at: https://www.justiceinspectorates.gov.uk/hmiprisons/wp-content/uploads/sites/4/2015/05/Tinsley-House-web-2014.pdf

HMIP '*Report on an Unannounced inspection of Yarl's Wood Immigration Removal Centre*' 2015 at: https://www.justiceinspectorates.gov.uk/hmiprisons/wp-content/uploads/sites/4/2015/08/Yarls-Wood-web-2015.pdf

Independent Chief Inspector of Borders and Immigration '*An inspection of the 'hostile environment' measures relating to driving licences and bank accounts*' (2016) https://assets.publishing.service.gov.uk/government/uploads/system/uploads/attachment_data/file/567652/ICIBI-hostile-environment-driving-licences-and-bank-accounts-January-to-July-2016.pdf

Independent Monitoring Board (IMB) '*Independent Monitoring Board Annual Report 2015 Dungavel House Immigration Removal Centre*' (2015) at: http://www.imb.org.uk/wp-content/uploads/2016/03/Dungavel-2015.pdf

IMB 'Annual Report 2015 Yarl's Wood Independent Monitoring Board' (2015) at: http://www.imb.org.uk/wp-content/uploads/2016/06/Yarls-Wood-IRC-2015.pdf

IMB '*Annual Report Independent Monitoring Board Colnbrook Immigration Removal Centre Now Part of Heathrow IRCs*'(2014) at: http://www.imb.org.uk/wp-content/uploads/2015/04/Colnbrook-2014.pdf

IMB '*Annual Report of the Board for The Verne Immigration Removal Centre*'(2015) at: http://www.imb.org.uk/wp-content/uploads/2016/05/The-Verne-2015.pdf

IMB '*Annual Report of the Independent Monitoring Board for Brook House Immigration Removal Centre*' (2015) at: http://www.imb.org.uk/wpcontent/uploads/2016/04/Brook-House-IRC-2015.pdf

IMB '*Annual Report: Harmondsworth Immigration Removal Centre*'(2014) at: http://www.imb.org.uk/wp-content/uploads/2015/04/Harmondsworth-IMB-Annual-Report-2014.pdf

IMB '*Annual Report: Heathrow Immigration Removal Centre*'(2015) at: http://www.imb.org.uk/wp-content/uploads/2016/05/Heathrow-IRC-2015.pdf

IMB '*Campsfield House Immigration Removal Centre Annual Report*'(2015) at: http://www.imb.org.uk/wp-content/uploads/2016/04/Campsfield-House-2015.pdf

IMB '*Cedars Pre-Departure Accommodation Independent Monitoring Board 2015 Annual Report*' (2015) at: http://www.imb.org.uk/wp-content/uploads/2016/05/Cedars-PDA-2015.pdf

IMB '*Tinsley House Immigration Removal Centre Independent Monitoring Board 2015 Annual Report*' (2015) at: http://www.imb.org.uk/wp-content/uploads/2016/05/Tinsley-House-IRC-2015.pdf

Lampard, K and Marsden, E '*Independent investigation into concerns about Yarl's Wood immigration removal centre*'(2016) Verita at: http://www.verita.net/wp-content/uploads/2016/04/Independent-investigation-into-concerns-about-Yarl%E2%80%99s-Wood-immigration-removal-centre-Serco-plc-Kate-Lampard-Ed-Marsden-January-2016.pdf

Newcomen, N '*Investigation into the death of a man on 10 February 2013 while a detainee at Harmondsworth Immigration Removal Centre*'(2015) at: http://www.ppo.gov.uk/wp-content/uploads/2015/10/H176-13-Death-of-a-male-detainee-in-hospital_Harmondsworth-IRC_10.02.13_Nat.pdf#view=FitH

Newspaper Articles

Bulman, M '*More than £500m spent on UK immigration detention over four years*' (2018) Independent at: https://www.independent.co.uk/news/uk/home-news/uk-immigration-detention-centre-cost-taxpayer-brexit-eu-migrants-a8195251.html

Channel 4 News '*Yarl's Wood: undercover in the secretive immigration centre*' (2015) at: http://www.channel4.com/news/yarls-wood-immigration-removal-detention-centre-investigation

Coates, S '*Labour and Tories back 28-day limit on immigrant detention*' (2019) The Times https://www.thetimes.co.uk/article/labour-and-tories-back-28-day-limit-on-immigrant-detention-qw3rrhh65

Dearden, L '*UN tells UK government to stop forcing NHS and landlords to enforce 'hostile environment'*' (2018) Independent at: https://www.independent.co.uk/news/uk/home-news/un-uk-nhs-landlords-immigration-hostile-environment-special-rapporteur-brexit-a8347481.html

Elgot, J and Taylor, M '*Calais crisis: Cameron condemned for 'dehumanising' description of migrants*' (2015) Guardian at: https://www.theguardian.com/uk-news/2015/jul/30/david-cameron-migrant-swarm-language-condemned

Farrer, M, Grierson, J and Sparrow, A '*Sajid Javid disowns 'hostile environment' phrase in first outing as home secretary*' (2018) Guardian at: https://www.theguardian.com/politics/live/2018/apr/30/theresa-may-new-home-secretary-amber-rudd-quits-politics-live

Fenton, S '*Home Office refuses to reveal whether women in Yarl's Wood have been raped in case it 'damages the commercial interests' of companies*' (2016) Independent at: http://www.independent.co.uk/news/uk/politics/home-office-refusing-to-reveal-whether-women-in-yarls-wood-have-been-raped-to-protect-the-commercial-a7077736.html

Kirkup, J and Winnett, R *'Theresa May interview: 'We're going to give illegal migrants a really hostile reception'* (2012) Telegraph at: http://www.telegraph.co.uk/news/uknews/immigration/9291483/Theresa-May-interview-Were-going-to-give-illegal-migrants-a-really-hostile-reception.html

Stone, J *'Government accused of scrapping pledge to end child detention in prison-style immigration removal centres'* (2016) Independent at: http://www.independent.co.uk/news/uk/politics/child-detention-immigration-centres-scrapped-broken-promise-tinsley-house-cedars-barnados-home-a7149981.html

Taylor, D, Walker, P and Grierson, J *'Revealed: two suicide attempts every day in UK deportation centres'* (2018) Guardian at: https://www.theguardian.com/uk-news/2018/oct/11/revealed-two-suicide-attempts-every-day-uk-deportation-detention-centres

Wright, O *'EU referendum: Nigel Farage's anti-migrant poster like 1930s fascist propaganda, says George Osborne'* (2016) Independent at: https://www.independent.co.uk/news/uk/politics/eu-referendum-poster-nigel-farage-polls-michael-gove-a7089946.html

'End the inhumanity of immigration detention' (2018) Guardian at: https://www.theguardian.com/uk-news/2018/mar/15/end-the-inhumanity-of-immigration-detention

Websites

Detention Forum *'Another 100 beds at Gatwick site: expansion by stealth?'* August 2016 at: http://detentionforum.org.uk/another-100-beds-at-gatwick-site-expansion-by-stealth/

Global Detention Project 'Immigration Detention in France' (2019) at: https://www.globaldetentionproject.org/countries/europe/france

Global Detention Project 'Immigration Detention in Germany' (2019) at: https://www.globaldetentionproject.org/countries/europe/germany

Global Detention Project 'Immigration Detention in Hungary' (2019) at: https://www.globaldetentionproject.org/countries/europe/hungary

Griffiths, M and Silverman, S *'Immigration Detention in the UK'* (2019) Migration Observatory at: https://migrationobservatory.ox.ac.uk/resources/briefings/immigration-detention-in-the-uk/

Home Affairs Committee *'Cavalier' Home Office failing in its responsibility for immigration detention'* (2019) at: https://www.parliament.uk/business/committees/committees-a-z/commons-select/home-affairs-committee/news-parliament-2017/immigration-detention-report-published-17-19/

JCWI *'Dossier of Failure - Windrush and the Hostile Environment'* (2018) at: https://www.jcwi.org.uk/news-and-policy/dossier-of-failure-windrush-and-hostile-environment

JCWI, '*What's next for the Hostile Environment: The Immigration Act 2016 and the Queen's Speech*' (2016) at: https://www.jcwi.org.uk/blog/2016/05/23/what%E2%80%99s-next-hostile-environment-immigration-act-2016-and-queen%E2%80%99s-speech

McKinney, Conor James '*Home Affairs Committee probes "systemic" problems with immigration detention*' Free Movement (2018) at: https://www.freemovement.org.uk/home-affairs-committee-probes-systemic-problems-in-immigration-detention/

Other

BBC Panoroma, '*Undercover: Britain's Immigration Secrets*' (2017) at: https://www.bbc.co.uk/programmes/b094mhsn

International Private Law as a Model for Private Law Jurisdiction in Cyberspace

Dr. P. R. Stephenson[1]

University of Leicester School of Law

Summary. This research explores a theory of cyber law expressed in the form of seven guidelines and based upon international principles of jurisdiction. Focus in cyberlaw largely has been on aspects of cybercrime rather than the theory, philosophy, and science of cyber law generally. This article seeks to characterize the jurisprudential aspects of cyber law jurisdiction by developing a broad measuring stick that can be applied to the law as it impacts cyberspace. The attention herein is on private law, and the primary focus is to begin to regularize a vocabulary that can be understood by both the legal and cyber communities, to develop guidelines for applying settled concepts in the physical space to the problem of jurisdiction in cyber space, and the development of new legal paradigms addressing yet unknown issues in cyber jurisprudence. These issues – vocabulary and jurisdiction - form the most significant stumbling blocks to the development of a coherent, universal, and useful jurisprudence addressing issues in cyber space, now and in the future.

The private law explored addressing private law jurisdiction is derived from international legal concepts. The landscape is viewed in three ways ("Law Types"): 1. Settled, physical space law; 2. Physical space law that can be molded or interpreted to address cyberspace; 3. Areas where new laws must be made to address issues that are uniquely cyber-related.

This article addresses some of the most relevant issues, resources and cases, both from the U.S. and internationally. It is not intended to be pervasive, but rather as a starting point for further discussion and research.

---

[1] Email: prs33@leicester.ac.uk

Keywords: cyberspace, cyber law, jurisdiction, international law, private law, cyber definitions

I. Introduction

Perhaps the easiest way to parse jurisdiction and choice of laws in cyberspace is to develop a framework that addresses, in general terms, all the possible permutations and combinations of cyber events and the venues in which they occur or, in some cases, pass through. Because of the unique nature of cyberspace events we should have an existing model to help us view the cyber landscape. For the purpose of this research we view the cyber landscape through the lens of international private law and accompanying rules and procedures. Equally important, this paper posits starting points for discussion based upon empirical observation, case review and additional resources. Much of its content is analysis of these resources and must, therefore, be considered subjective. The results of these analyses are summarized in a set of seven Guidelines for determining proper jurisdiction in cyberspace based upon the four Constructs and three Law Types.

International events share similarities with cyberspace events in several ways. First, they may occur completely within the jurisdiction of a single forum. Second, they may occur in a single forum and pass through another jurisdiction. Finally, they may begin in one jurisdiction and end in another. On the surface, at least, the venues appear borderless. It often is said of cyberspace that it is borderless but that may not necessarily be true[2]. Under some circumstances – such as events that are contained within a single jurisdiction – forum and cyber borders are the same.

In cyberspace, there are some interesting permutations of these possibilities. Perhaps the most significant of these is the differentiation between human-caused events and autonomous events. The most obvious of autonomous events in the physical world is the autonomous vehicle. Currently, in the United States, California, Nevada, Michigan and Florida have statutes relating to autonomous vehicles[3].The cyber version of an autonomous vehicle is an autonomous program referred to as a "bot" (robot). An autonomous bot would be capable of learning and making decisions on its own based upon its programming rather than under the direct guidance of a human ("bot herder") or a command and control

[2] Michael N. Schmitt, Tallinn manual 2.0 on the international law applicable to cyber operations (Prepared by the International Groups of Experts at the Invitation of the NATO Cooperative Cyber Defence Centre of Excellence 2 ed. 2017).

[3] Unmanned Systems in Homeland Security. (2015).

server. In the physical world, autonomous vehicles are manufactured by known entities and both the entity and the vehicles undergo examination and special licensing. If an autonomous event occurs involving the vehicle, there is a manufacturer and software developer that can be held accountable.

In the cyber world it is very likely that the developer of a bot – usually a criminal hacker – will not be known. So, we must divide the events in the cyber world into two broad categories: those under human control and autonomous events. Within these broad categories we must account for four types of events. However, both behave similarly. Although there are subtleties in the degree and type of autonomous behavior, those technical details are beyond the scope of this paper. Also, within our framework we must account for two specific types of jurisdiction and procedure: Forum Jurisdiction (Private Law and Civil Procedure), and International Jurisdiction (Private Law and Civil Procedure). From these two types we may derive a third type: Cyberspace-derived Jurisdiction (Private Law and Civil Procedure). This means that, being guided and informed by the applicable type of jurisdiction, we may derive a guideline for jurisdiction in cyberspace that addresses the event types discussed below, both for human-involved events and autonomous events.

II. Types of Cyber Events

There are four general types of cyber events from the perspective of jurisdiction in the cyberspace:

> **Construct 1**: The event is completely within the forum's jurisdiction. It begins and ends in the forum without passing through any other jurisdiction.
>
> **Construct 2**: The cyber event begins and ends in the same forum's jurisdiction but at some point, it passes through another jurisdiction
>
> **Construct 3**: The event begins in one jurisdiction and ends in another without any intermediate stops in other jurisdictions.
>
> **Construct 4**: The event begins in one jurisdiction and ends in another but makes intermediate stops in a third (or more) jurisdiction(s).

As long as these events are human-controlled, we can identify important touchstones such as who commenced the event and who the target was. For example, in a hacking incident we can (often) identify the alleged hacker and we can identify the victim. Intellectual property cases have similar characteristics from the standpoint of jurisdictions. When we are faced with an autonomous event those touchstones likely disappear. However, that does not alter the jurisdictional issues. It simply makes attribution more difficult.

III. Analysis

1. Historical Background

Stephenson[4] quotes three postulates for solving conflict of laws issues from Huber[5] (from the 1600s):

1. The laws of each state have force within the limits of that government and bind all subjects to it, but not beyond.
2. All persons within the limits of a government, whether they live there permanently or temporarily, are deemed to be subjects thereof.
3. Sovereigns will so act by way of comity that rights acquired within the limits of a government retain their force everywhere so far as they do not cause prejudice to the power or rights of such government or of its subjects.

The notion of the "place of the wrong" appears to offer a starting point for placing jurisdiction[6]:

> The place of wrong is in the state where the last event necessary to make an actor liable for an alleged tort takes place[7].

Rule 4 of the "First Restatement" (footnote 4) gives us a bit of guidance when fraud is involved. Fraud is a common act in cyberspace, so this rule

---

4 Peter R. Stephenson, Jurisdiction in Cyberspace: A Question of Conflict of Laws? (2018).

5 Jack Goldsmith Lea Brilmayer, Erin O'Hara O'Connor, Conflict of Law - Cases and Materials (Wolters Kluwer 7 ed. 2015).

6 Within this paper we will use the terms "place of the harm" and "place of the wrong" interchangeably, recognizing that there may be subtle contextual differences in some cases.

7 American Law Institute, Restatement (First) of Conflict of Laws § 377 (American Law Institute. 1934).

has its points of interest. Chief among these is a refinement of the place of the wrong specific to fraud:

> 'Rule 4. When a person sustains a loss by fraud, the place of wrong is **where the loss is sustained**, **not where the fraudulent representations are made**.' (emphasis added)

The "First Restatement" also gives us some insight as to what it means by the place of the wrong. Note he consistency with the interpretation above:

> '… the place of the wrong is the place where the **last event necessary to make an actor liable** for an alleged tort takes place.' (emphasis added)

The "First Restatement" was Updated[8] in 1971 and significantly it updated the place of the wrong to be subservient to the most significant relationship. The "Second Restatement" (footnote 8) states in relevant part:

> (1) A court, subject to constitutional restrictions, will follow a statutory directive of its own state on choice of law.
> (2) When there is no such directive, the factors relevant to the choice of the applicable rule of law include
> (a) the needs of the interstate and international systems,
> (b) the relevant policies of the forum,
> (c) the relevant policies of other interested states and the relative interests of those states in the determination of the particular issue,
> (d) the protection of justified expectations,
> (e) the basic policies underlying the particular field of law,
> (f) certainty, predictability and uniformity of result, and
> (g) ease in the determination and application of the law to be applied.

Generally, this defines the significant relationship test. However, both the place of the wrong – Lex Loci Delicti – and the most significant relationship tests are American and may or may not work well in an international event. While the United States may be inclined to accept these principles, there is no guarantee that any other nation – particularly those without applicable treaties with the US – will operate under their guidance. However, there is guidance on an international scale from the "Tallinn Manu-

[8] American Law Institute, Restatement (Second) of Conflict of Laws § 6 (American Law Institute. 1971).

al"[9]. The Manual's Rule 1 – Sovereignty (general principle)[10] says, in relevant part: "The principle of state sovereignty applies in cyberspace." (emphasis added) While the first version of the Manual addressed cyber war, the second version – the one quoted – expands that coverage to include general principles in cyberspace law, going beyond cyber warfare.

The Manual eschews the notion of a "...global common", or "...global domain or fifth domain that lacks physicality and is virtual in nature" in favor of reverting to the principles of sovereignty noting that:

> Cyber activities occur on territory and involve objects, or are conducted by persons or entities, over which States may exercise their sovereign prerogatives. In particular, the Experts noted that although cyber activities may cross multiple borders, or occur in international waters, international airspace, or outer space, all are conducted by individuals or entities subject to the jurisdiction of one or more States.

The Manual's Rule 2 addresses internal sovereignty which refers to "... sovereign authority with regard to the cyber infrastructure, persons, and cyber activities located within its territory, subject to its international legal obligations."

Similarly, Rule 3 addresses external sovereignty which the Manual defines as a State's freedom "...to conduct cyber activities in its international relations, subject to any contrary rule of international law binding it." These rules form a platform upon which States are expected to relate to each other in cyberspace. The Manual, however, is in the form of an analysis rather than settled law. Still, it offers a basis for exploring jurisdictional issues in cyberspace. We will consider the two Restatements and the Tallinn Manual as starting points for the development of a framework of jurisdictional guidelines for cyberspace.

---

9 Schmitt, 2017.

10 "A number of principles and rules of conventional and customary international law derive from the general principle of sovereignty. Examples include those relating to jurisdiction (Chapter 3), including the obligation to respect certain immunities of other States (Rule 5), and the principle of due diligence (Rule 6)."

a. Exploring Stare Decisis[11]

Because there is little legislative law in the United States that addresses cyber law – especially civil law – directly, we depend heavily on case, or "judge-made" law. We begin this section by looking at a few seminal cases in the United States and then move on to international cases. Some of these cases refer to issues that provided a background for interpreting existing legislative law. Such is the first case discussed here.

b. Reno v. American Civil Liberties Union et al[12]

This case struck down portions of the Act that prohibited "…transmission of obscene or indecent communications by means of telecommunications device to persons under age 18" as imposing restrictions on free speech in general and was overbroad in its interpretation of the First Amendment to the US Constitution. The importance of this case is very broad, for example, affecting content in general on the Internet. Today we see everything from child pornography to terrorist recruitment on the World Wide Web. The Court held that, "…The CDA's "indecent transmission" and "patently offensive display" provisions abridge "the freedom of speech" protected by the First Amendment". This has had wide-ranging impact on cases involving freedom of speech on the Internet.

c. Zeran v. America Online[13]

This case set a very important stake in the ground: web sites can host third party content without being responsible for it. The Court held that America Online (AOL) did not have the responsibility to police indepen-

[11] The first five (a-e) cases identified courtesy of "The Verge" - These six lawsuits shaped the internet https://www.theverge.com/2014/8/19/6044679/the-six-lawsuits-that-shaped-the-internet.

[12] Plaintiffs filed suit challenging constitutionality of provisions of the Communications Decency Act (CDA) provisions seeking to protect minors from harmful material on the Internet Reno v. Am. Civil Liberties Union, 521 U.S. 844, 117 S. Ct. 2329, 138 L. Ed. 2d 874 (1997)117 S. Ct. 2329 Supreme Court of the United States, Janet RENO, Attorney General of the United States, et al., Appellants v. American Civil Liberties Union et al.

[13] Negligence action was brought against commercial interactive computer service provider alleging that provider unreasonably delayed in removing defamatory messages posted by unidentified third party, refused to post retractions of those messages, and failed to screen for similar postings thereafter. Zeran v. Am. Online, Inc., 129 F.3d 327 (4th Cir. 1997) 129 F.3d 327 United States Court of Appeals, Fourth Circuit. Kenneth M. Zeran, Plaintiff–Appellant, v. America Online, Incorporated, Defendant–Appellee. Argued Oct. 2, 1997.Decided Nov. 12, 1997.

dent third parties who posted defamatory or indecent materials on an AOL web site. Zeran, who sued AOL because a prank posted on a web site hosted by AOL defamed him. The Court ruled that the CDA bars Zeran's claims.

d. Zippo Manufacturing Company v. Zippo Dot Com, Inc.

This is perhaps the best-known classical American cyber law case[14]. Its importance lies in its role in shaping the application of personal jurisdiction in cyberspace. To that extent it forms a useful historical touch-stone for our research[15]. Zippo Manufacturing Company is the maker of Zippo lighters, with its headquarters in Bradford, Pennsylvania. Zippo Dot Com was an internet news service located in Sunnyvale, California. The case turns on Manufacturing's complaint that Dot Com has infringed Manufacturing's trademarks and other similar claims. The claims were both Federal and based upon Pennsylvania law. Dot Com set a motion before the Court for dismissal based upon lack of jurisdiction in Pennsylvania since Dot Com was a California company. Dot Com also moved to relocate the case to another Federal Court under 28 U.S.C. § 1406(a)[16]. The Court denied the motion. The court held that:

> (1) service purposefully availed itself of doing business in Pennsylvania and thus could be subject to personal jurisdiction there;
> (2) action arose out of service's forum-related conduct;
> (3) exercise of jurisdiction in Pennsylvania would be reasonable; and,
> (4) venue was proper.

---

[14] Zippo Mfg. Co. v. Zippo Dot Com, Inc., 952 F. Supp. 1119 (W.D. Pa. 1997) 952 F.Supp. 1119 United States District Court, W.D. Pennsylvania. Zippo Manufacturing Company, Plaintiff, v. Zippo Dot Com, Inc., Defendant. Jan. 16, 1997.

[15] The "Zippo Test" Has been debated widely based upon its apparent simplicity in an environment – the Internet – that is anything but simple. See, for example: Pres-Kap, Inc. v. System One, Direct Access, Inc., 636 So. 2d 1351 (Fla. App. 3 Dist. 1994), CompuServe, Inc. v. Patterson, 89 F.3d 1257 (6th Cir. 1996), Cybersell, Inc. v. Cybersell, Inc., 130 F.3d 414 (9th Cir. 1997) and Dudnikov v. Chalk & Vermilion, 514 F.3d 1063 (10th Cir. 2008) (Note the Court's use of the "5-part effects test" from Calder v. Jones, 465 U.S. 783 (1984) for personal jurisdiction in Dudnikov).

[16] "(a) The district court of a district in which is filed a case laying venue in the wrong division or district shall dismiss, or if it be in the interest of justice, transfer such case to any district or division in which it could have been brought."

This case tests two things. Specifically, it tests the constitutionality of Pennsylvania's long-arm statute. Generally, it tests application of personal jurisdiction over the Internet. While Dot Com was, indeed, a California company, it did approximately 2% of its business in Pennsylvania and it required explicit subscriber sign-up, showing clearly that Dot Com knew that it was doing business in Pennsylvania and continued to do so. Thus, the Court ruled that the venue as proper.

e. ProCD v. Zeidenberg[17]

In this case the defendant purchased a list of phone numbers from the plaintiff and then made those data available to the public for a price somewhat below that of the plaintiff. The defendant claimed that the plaintiff's copyright was invalid since phone numbers – and therefore lists of phone numbers – cannot be copyright. Therefore, since there can be no copyright, there could be no copyright violation. The court found that this was not a copyright issue but a straightforward contract issue. Since the defendant had clicked through numerous notifications of license terms and accepted them, rather than violating the copyright, he breached the contract. The District Court held that the license agreement constituted a contract which was itself enforceable under standard contract law. The importance of this case is that shrink wrap licenses are enforceable as contracts where both parties have agreed to the terms. This also applies to online licenses and terms of use[18]. Perhaps more important to our research, it teaches that some apparent "cyber cases" are, in fact, simple cases that can be addressed by settled law and legal norms. The decision was reversed by the Court of Appeals.

---

[17] Shrink-wrap licenses are enforceable unless their terms are objectionable on grounds applicable to contracts in general (for example, if they violate a rule of positive law, or if they are unconscionable ProCD, Inc. v. Zeidenberg, 86 F.3d 1447 (7th Cir. 1996).

[18] See, for example, CoStar Realty Information, Inc. v. Field: "...a user's affirmative act of clicking an "Agree" button in order to enter the website binds the user to the Terms of Use associated with using the website".

f. Religious Technology Center v. Netcom On-Line Communication Services, Inc.[19]

This case establishes the copyright infringement liability for situations where a website connects to the material of another website. The plaintiffs held copyrights to unpublished works of L. Ron Hubbard. One defendant was a frequent contributor to the alt.religion.scientology ("a.r.s.") newsgroup on the Internet. He linked a bulletin board system ("BBS") owned by another defendant where copies of Hubbard's manuscripts were available without direct authorization of the copyright holders. The BBS gained access to the Internet through Netcom On-Line Communications Services, the third defendant. Plaintiff alleges copyright infringement, among other things, by Netcom, for allowing the posting of copyright material owned by Plaintiff. The court held that Netcom could not be held liable for material posted on sites owned by its subscribers.

g. Pres-Kap, Inc. v. System One, Direct Access, Inc[20]

This takes Zippo a step further. While Zippo addressed users of a website located in a different jurisdiction, Pres-Kap deals with contracts between a supplier of computing and networks services under contract to a user in a different jurisdiction. Unlike the Zippo court, the Pres-Kap court held that a contract that crosses jurisdictional boundaries is not sufficient to

---

[19] Copyright holders brought infringement action against operator of computer bulletin board service (BBS) and Internet access provider, seeking to hold defendants liable for copyright infringement committed by BBS subscriber. Access provider filed motion for summary judgment, operator filed motion for judgment on the pleadings, and holders filed motion for preliminary injunction. The District Court, Whyte, J., held that: (1) access provider was not directly liable for copies that were made and stored on its computer Religious Tech. Ctr. v. Netcom On-Line Commc'n Servs., Inc., 907 F. Supp. 1361 United States District Court, N.D. California. Religious Technology Centre, a California non-profit corporation; and Bridge Publications, Inc., a California non-profit corporation, Plaintiffs, v. Netcom On–Line Communication Services, Inc., a Delaware corporation; Dennis Erlich, an individual; and Tom Klemesrud, an individual, dba Clearwood Data Services, Defendants. Nov. 21, 1995.

[20] Computer system lessor brought action against lessee for breach of lease after lessee stopped making payments. The Circuit Court, Dade County, Robert P. Kaye, J., denied lessee's motion to dismiss for lack of personal jurisdiction. Lessee appealed. The District Court of Appeal, Hubbart, J., held that lessee had insufficient minimum contacts for exercise of personal jurisdiction Pres-Kap, Inc. v. Sys. One, Direct Access, Inc., 636 So.2d 1351 (Fla. Dist. Ct. App. 1994) District Court of Appeal of Florida.

establish minimum contacts[21] for determining personal jurisdiction. This is an important case because it establishes that remote usage of a system (for example, over the Internet), is insufficient to trigger personal jurisdiction. Comparing this case with Zippo shows that the Zippo case involved issues not covered by Pres-Kap. For example, Zippo Dot Com knew of, but ignored, the fact that many of its subscribers were located in Pennsylvania, the forum state for Zippo Manufacturing. In Pres-Kap the contractee simply participated in a contract with a remote contractor.

Considering "the place of the wrong" as a key element to establishing personal jurisdiction, we find that the place of the alleged wrong is in New York where the System One servers apparently failed to trigger a stop payment and suit for breach by Pres-Kap. However, the Pres-Kap court found that the constitutional issue of due process played a key –

[21] The minimum contacts test in the United States derives from U.S. Supreme Court, International Shoe v. State of Washington, 326 U.S. 310 (1945) where the Court held that a salesman with a large amount of business in Washington state was subject to state withholding tax, even though he worked for a foreign corporation, due to the large number of contacts within Washington. In Shaffer v. Heitner, 433 U.S. 186 (1977) the Court held that, "Whether or not a State can assert jurisdiction over a nonresident must be evaluated according to the minimum contacts standard of International Shoe Co. v. Washington", "…and thus the focus shifted to the relationship among the defendant, the forum, and the litigation, rather than the mutually exclusive sovereignty of the States…" Justia, US Supreme Court, https://supreme.justia.com/cases/federal/us/433/186/ Additionally, see Calder v. Jones, 465 U. S. 783 (1984) where the Court held, "… 2.(a) The Due Process Clause permits personal jurisdiction over a defendant in any State with which the defendant has "certain minimum contacts . . . such that the maintenance of the suit does not offend 'traditional notions of fair play and substantial justice.'" This addresses the place of the harm and has become known as the Effects Test. While this largely is a U. S. construct, it is also found internationally and can be a factor in determining jurisdiction in the Internet.

even deciding – role[22]. Relevant International law suggests that, while US courts interpret the "minimum contacts" standard when dealing with foreign jurisdictions, European courts tend to equate personal jurisdiction with the residence of the defendant[23].

h. The Case of the S.S. "Lotus" (France v. Turkey)

The S.S. Lotus case has become a touchstone of international private law jurisdiction since it was decided by the Permanent Court of International Justice (PCIJ) in September of 1927. This case established a principle of international law (henceforth referred to as the Lotus Principle). Essentially, the Lotus Principle says that a sovereign nation may act in whatever way it wishes as long as no standing, accepted international laws, treaties or principles contravene its actions[24]. The S. S. Lotus was a French steamship and the S. S. Bozkurt was Turkish. There was a collision between the Lotus and The Bozkurt in which eight Turkish sailors died. The accident occurred in neutral waters. Turkey claimed jurisdiction to try the French watch officer at the time of the crash. France claimed jurisdiction since the officer was on a ship flying the French flag. The Court did not agree and awarded jurisdiction to Turkey[25]. Judge Moore, referring to the PCIJ Lotus Case, was clear on what became the

[22] "The law is well settled that in order for a state court to subject a nonresident defendant to an *in personam* judgment, due process requires that the nonresident defendant have certain minimum contacts with the forum state such that the suit does not offend traditional maintenance of the notions of fair play and substantial justice. ... In the instant case, the record clearly shows that the defendant is a New York corporation doing business in New York as a travel agency with no offices outside of New York; that the plaintiff, through its New York office, solicited the defendant's business in the state of New York where the subject contract, as well as prior contracts, were negotiated by the parties and executed by the defendant; that the computer equipment supplied under the contract was delivered to the defendant in New York; and when the defendant experienced difficulties with the computerized equipment, complaints were directed to the New York office of the plaintiff." - Pres-Kap, Inc. v. System One, Direct Access, Inc.

[23] Cedric Ryngaert, Jurisdiction in International Law (Oxford University Press. 2008).

[24] Wikipedia, Lotus Case, Wikipedia (2009). (verified internal references – "Publication of the Permanent Court of International Justice Series A. No. 10 September 7th, 1927 Collection of Judgements - The Case of the S.S. Lotus" (English translation))

[25] For incidents on the high seas, this ruling has been contradicted by article 11, 1958 High Seas Convention which states that the flag state of the vessel or the nationality of the accused determines the forum State.

Lotus Principle was applicable[26]. This principle, of course, complicates the jurisdiction issue once jurisdictions outside of the United States are involved.

i. Erich Gasser GmbH v MISAT Srl[27]

Sancho Villa[28] analyzes international jurisdiction issues and refers to the Gasser case as one example of choice of venue. The Gasser case is especially interesting since it involves two States, both of which claimed jurisdiction. Gasser was an Austrian company while MISAT Srl was an Italian company. MISAT sued in the Italian court over a contract dispute. Gasser retaliated with a suit in the Austrian court over non-payment of its invoices by MISAT. Gasser's position was that the parties had agreed on the basis of Gasser's invoices containing a choice of jurisdiction to which MISAT never disputed. For several reasons MISAT claimed that the Italian court had jurisdiction, the most relevant to jurisdiction in cyber space being that article 2 of the Brussels Convention of 1968[29] awarded jurisdiction to the State where the defendant was domiciled.

This is not consistent with the First Restatement and Zippo, in the United States. In both instances the place of the wrong is the place where the impact was felt. In Gasser, the harm was felt in Austria and in MISAT

---

26 Judge Moore in the case of The S. S. Lotus in the judgment of the Permanent Court of International Justice of 7 September 1927, France v Turkey, Series A, No. 10, p. 69 according to which: "... the principle of absolute and exclusive jurisdiction within national territory applies to foreigners as well as to citizens or inhabitants, and the foreigner can claim no exemption from the exercise of such jurisdiction, except in so far as he may be able to show either: ..." However, the Lotus Principle was later overruled for events at sea by the 1958 High Seas Convention, Article 11(1). This does not impact its value as a principle in cyberlaw.

27 Erich Gasser GmbH v Misat Srl (C-116/02) European Court of Justice 09 December 2003.

28 Diana Sancho Villa, Jurisdiction Over Jurisdiction and Choice of Court Agreements: Views on the Hague Convention of 2005 and Implications for the European Regime, 12 Yearbook of Private International Law, (2010).

29 1968 Brussels Convention on jurisdiction and the enforcement of judgments in civil and commercial matters. While Article 2 establishes primary jurisdiction as the domicile of the defendant, however "...for torts, delicts or quasi-delicts, the Regulation establishes the alternative jurisdiction of the **place where the harmful event occurred or may occur** (Article 5, number 3). This rule has been interpreted as including both the place where the damage occurred and the place where the harmful event happened, taking into account the initial direct damage, but not the consequential damages." – emphasis added http://www.bankpedia.org/index.php/en/87-english/b/23146-brussels-convention-encyclopedia.

it was felt in Italy. However, Internationally the results were the reverse, granting jurisdiction to the State where the defendant was domiciled – the MISAT suit being Austria where Gasser (defendant) resided and the Gasser suit being Italy where MISAT (defendant) resided. However, note footnote 29; Article 5 establishes the place of the wrong in some circumstances as the court of jurisdiction for certain types of actions. Gasser was, essentially, a contract dispute rather than the type of tort that Article 5 anticipates.

2. Complications, Conflicts and Contradictions

a. Territorial and Extraterritorial Jurisdiction

Simply, the territorial principle states that the location of an act determines jurisdiction. So an act committed in France, regardless of the nationalities of the actors, is under French jurisdiction. The extraterritorial principle extends, in effect, a forum's jurisdiction outside of the confines of the forum. The common expression of this is personal jurisdiction where a State seeks to extradite one of its citizens to face charges in his or her home venue rather than the venue where the act was committed. An extension of that is request for evidence gathering in the venue where the act took place by the venue where the actor resides.

Judge Learned Hand, speaking for the United States declared that:

> It is settled law […] that any state may impose liabilities [may exercise jurisdiction over] even upon persons not within its allegiance, for conduct outside its borders that the consequences within its borders for which the state reprehends, and these liabilities other states will ordinarily recognize[30].

This certainly comports with extraterritoriality and harks back to the notion of "place of the harm". Retrieving evidence from one State by the courts of another generally depends on comity. This level of cooperation is especially common in Europe[31]. Comity is defined as:

> … the courts of one state or jurisdiction giving effect to laws and judicial decisions of another state or jurisdiction, not as

---

30 United States v. Aluminum Co. of Am., 148 F.2d 416 Circuit Court of Appeals, Second Circuit. United States v. Aluminum Co. of America et al. March 12, 1945.

31 Ryngaert. 2008.

> a matter of obligation but out of deference and mutual respect[32].

b. Genuine Connection

The notion of genuine connection is not well-defined in international law:

> No absolute test of the "genuine connection" has found general acceptance. Such tests as have been applied are of a relative nature and sometimes links with one State have had to be weighed against those of another[33].

Striving for a genuine connection in international private cyberlaw well could become an exercise in futility, especially where traffic over the Internet – some of it autonomous – is concerned.

IV. Deriving a Framework for Cyberspace Jurisdiction

We begin the derivation of a framework for jurisdiction in cyberspace by examining and important touchstone: the *subsidiarity principle.* Ryngaert expounds upon the *subsidiarity principle*[34] [35]. This is a test of reasonableness and will form the pedestal upon which our framework stands. At its core this principle says that the State with the strongest nexus to the case not only *may* but *must* exercise jurisdiction in a reasonable manner under the penalty of the other State taking control. Building upon subsidiarity, such concepts as *place of the wrong* begin to take shape in cyberspace. While the United States case law is not as useful for precedent outside, as it is within, the US, such case law can inform the framework for cyberspace law.

---

[32] Bryan A. Garner, Black's Law Dictionary (West Publishing Company 6 ed. 1990).

[33] Case Concerning Barcelona Traction, Light, and Power Company, Ltd [1970] ICJ.

[34] Ryngaert. 2008.

[35] "…a State may only exercise its jurisdiction if another State with a purportedly stronger nexus to the case fails to do so in ways that are reasonably acceptable to the would-be regulating State or to the international community at large. […] States with the strongest nexus to the case forfeit their right of protest against the other States' jurisdictional assertions over that case, if the former States fail to adequately deal with it." Ryngaert.

We recall from Section II that there are four ways that a cyber event could occur:

- **Case 1** - An event begun and completed totally within a forum.
- **Case 2** - An event begun in and ended in a forum but that passes through another forum in the process.
- **Case 3** - An event that is begun in one forum and completed in another forum having passed through but without stopping in a third (or more) forum.
- **Case 4** - An event begun in one forum and completed in another having stopped and restarted in a third (or more) forum.

This means that any useful framework must identify with each of the ways a cyber event could occur. Recall from earlier that there are three Constructs for cyberlaw.

- **Construct 1:** Well-settled law that fits well in cyberspace – e.g., an event that looks like it needs cyberlaw but really is a physical space type of case such as a contract issue.
- **Construct 2:** Well-settled law that could be interpreted in the context of cyberspace.
- **Construct 3:** A cyber event that requires a new law molded explicitly to the needs and restraints of cyberspace.

Each level of our framework must accommodate at least one of the constructs directly and must address all three as guidance. Looking over the guidance and seminal cases cited above we can begin to see some useful touchstones that may or may not help build a framework.

- Place of the wrong
- Subsidiarity Principle
- Rule 4 of the First Restatement
- Rules 1, 2 and 3 of the Tallinn Manual
- The Lotus Principle
- Zeran v. America Online
- Zippo Manufacturing Company v. Zippo Dot Com, Inc.

1. Place of the wrong

The place of the wrong is intuitive for cyber actions that begin and end in the same jurisdiction. Likewise, Pres-Kap teaches that in the United States personal jurisdiction usually is tied to the minimum contacts principle while European courts generally consider domicile. Since neither of these conditions is met for an event beginning and ending in the same jurisdiction after passing through another without stopping (e.g., the normal data flow through the core routers on the Internet), the place of the wrong continues to be the jurisdiction where the event has begun and ended. When an event begins in one forum and ends in another after passing through a third without stopping, the place of the wrong may be determined by settled physical space law. There is no special law required simply because the Internet was the delivery mechanism.

The final Case (4) – an event beginning in one forum and ending in another while passing through a third (or more) and stopping poses more cyber-related challenges. We do, however, have some guidelines. Rule 4 of the First Restatement teaches that in the case of fraud, the place of the wrong is where the impact of the fraud occurred. Otherwise it is the place where the last act necessary to complete the offense occurred[36].

a. A Fictitious Example Case

An actor on a cyber-crime website in Russia offers to sell a piece of malware. A second actor buys the malware and attacks a bank in the United States with it causing a million dollars in damage. Cyber investigators trace the attack and find that it came from a server in the Amazon network cloud. Examination of that server showed that it was compromised by an actor from a server in The Ukraine. There the trail appears to stop. Investigation of the Ukraine server shows that it is part of a hidden network[37]. Intelligence suggests that the server on the hidden network is responsible for tens of millions of dollars in on-line fraud. An actor – allegedly living in the Czech Republic is associated with the server but his real name and identity are unknown. This is an example of a case

[36] American Law Institute, Restatement (First) of Conflict of Laws § 377. (1934).

[37] Such networks sometimes are called "bullet-proof hosting" networks. See for example, the description on the Digital Shadows web site: "[…] bulletproof hosters provide protected internet infrastructure for serving up illicit content, whether that be malware command and control servers, phishing pages, online shops selling stolen credit cards, money-mule recruitment sites or in fact, most other online criminal schemes." https://www.digitalshadows.com/blog-and-research/criminal-services-bulletproof-hosting/

where the act started in one jurisdiction (arguably Ukraine), stops in another (Amazon in the US), and ends at the bank in the US, but in another jurisdiction from the physical location of the Amazon server of Amazon's lace of business.

b. Place of the Harm Analysis

The minimum contacts principle sets the personal jurisdiction over the actor as Ukraine since he or she operated from the network located there. However, European courts are more likely to place it in the Czech Republic where the actor allegedly resides. Using the guidelines of Rule 4, if the event was perpetration of a fraud, the place of the harm is where the impact occurred. That of course is the bank. If the act was not considered under a theory of fraud, the place of the wrong becomes the place where the Amazon server is located. Given these facts, a US court likely would claim personal jurisdiction over the actor. This is not dissimilar from a US case currently working its way through the US courts[38] as reported by Stephenson in an unpublished research paper. "On 22 December 2017 Microsoft Corporation (MS) filed a lawsuit[39] (the "complaint") in the United States District Court for the Western District of Washington at Seattle". [40]

Analysis of the network traffic involved showed that the likely source was, in Microsoft's view, a Comcast server located in Florida while Microsoft is located in Washington state. Microsoft claimed personal juris-

[38] A Jurisdictional Analysis of Microsoft v. 10 John Does Using IP Address 73.21.204.220. (2018).

[39] Microsoft Corporation v. John Does 1-10 using IP address73.21.204.220, (United States District Court, Western Disctrict of Washington at Seattle).

[40] "The suit alleges large-scale copyright infringement through software piracy and trademark infringement relative to Microsoft registered trademarks. What was unusual about this filing is that MS, at the time of filing, had nothing more on which to base its lawsuit than an IP address that had communicated over 28,000 times with its registration servers in Seattle." Stephenson

diction[41] based upon several precedent cases and ends by citing 28 USC 1391(b)[42]:

> We may note, therefore, that the place of the harm is the Western District of Washington and since the fraud was against Microsoft servers located there the minimum contacts principle was also satisfied. There are, of course, some technical considerations. For example, suppose that the actor was a resident of an island in the Caribbean not part of the US. Or, perhaps, as in our fictitious example, the actor was somewhere else in the world using a chain of several servers that ended in the Florida server.

Should it turn out to be the case that the actor(s) resided outside of the United States, however, Microsoft would be able to resort to the same section of the United States Code, this time citing paragraph (f)(1)[43]. This case was filed with the purpose of forcing Comcast to provide technical information from its server so that Microsoft could answer those questions.

2. The Lotus Principle

The Lotus Principle is one of the most often cited principles in international jurisdictional disputes. It states simply that a sovereign State can act as it pleases as long as no other laws or treaties are contravened. This would seem to make things simple. A State could simply claim jurisdiction based upon whatever legal standards it maintains and the venue

[41] "Venue is also proper in this district pursuant to 28 U.S.C. 1391(b) because a substantial part of the events giving rise to the claims occurred in the Western District of Washington."

[42] **(b) Venue in general.** –A civil action may be brought in–

(1) a judicial district in which any defendant resides, if all defendants are residents of the State in which the district is located; **(2)** a judicial district in which a substantial part of the events or omissions giving rise to the claim occurred, or a substantial part of property that is the subject of the action is situated; or **(3)** if there is no district in which an action may otherwise be brought as provided in this section, any judicial district in which any defendant is subject to the court's personal jurisdiction with respect to such action.

[43] **(f) Civil actions against a foreign state**--A civil action against a foreign state as defined in section 1603(a) of this title may be brought-- **(1)** in any judicial district in which a substantial part of the events or omissions giving rise to the claim occurred, or a substantial part of property that is the subject of the action is situated; …

would be settled. However, the place of the wrong may interpose difficulties in cyberspace. In our fictitious example, some of the involved countries simply could refuse to cooperate. Russia rarely cooperates in the investigation of cyber events, for example. The Lotus Principle, therefore, is not likely to be an adequate starting point for a cyber event.

The United States typically has taken the Microsoft approach above and claimed personal jurisdiction on multiple theories, both *stare decesis* and statutory. Under the subsidiarity principle should the US not proceed against the actor, any other impacted state could. Conversely, should Ukraine be determined as the venue, and Ukraine refused to proceed, the United States could assume jurisdiction and act in the case.

3. The Tallinn Manual

The Tallinn Manual gives us some guidelines that, because they have achieved some level of international authoritative guidance in actions taken in cyberspace, are likely to pose acceptable starting points for discussion. Particularly, Rule 1 states that States have jurisdiction over events occurring within their borders or involving persons over which they have sovereign jurisdiction. Rule 3 says that States may exercise their legal options as long as they stay within the boundaries of international laws and treaties.

V. Complexity, Emergence and Entropy: Concepts That Inform the Law in Jurisdictionally Complicated Analyses

Referring to Case 1, Case 2, Case 3 and Case 4 *supra* (Section II), and Constructs 1 – 3 (Abstract), we see combinations that are easy and combinations that are hard. For example, Case 1, where an event begins and ends within the same jurisdiction, combined with Construct 1, where there are adequate laws within the forum to address the issues, offers little or no challenge. However, Case 4, where an event begins in one jurisdiction and ends in another while passing through and stopping at intermediate jurisdictions, combined with Construct 2 or Construct 3 – both requiring cyber interpretation on some level – offers a complicated set of issues.

If, as in the Microsoft case[44], the defendant(s) take intentional measures to remain unidentifiable those issues become more complicated still. For addressing such complicated instances some technical analysis may be borrowed from science and mathematics. In describing the con-

[44] See footnote 39.

tributions these concepts may make to the law, we have attempted to focus upon the core cyber-legal issues without stripping the concepts completely of their scientific or mathematical meaning while avoiding those analyses that are peculiar to the concept outside of its benefit to the law.

1. Shannon Information Theory[45]

In 1948, Charles Shannon posed a theory of communication subsequently known as the Shannon Information Theory. In his paper he described a communication system as having six components:

- An information source
- A transmitter
- A communications channel
- A source of noise
- A receiver
- A destination

Diagrammatically this looks like this:

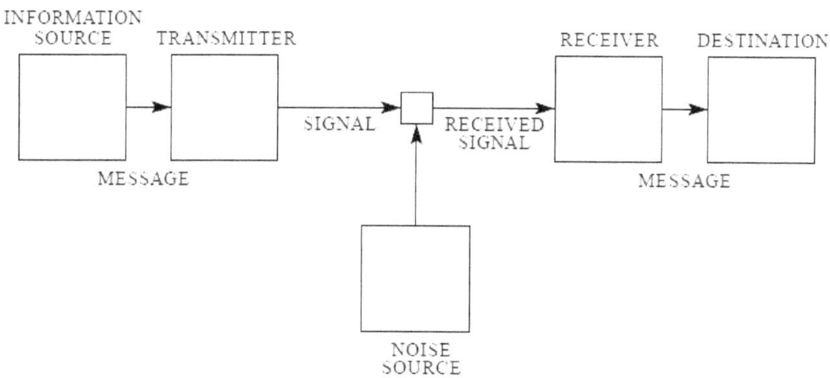

Figure 1 - The Shannon Information Model

In a simple Case 1/Construct 1 event the source (defendant) and destination (plaintiff) are clear and there is no – or very limited - noise source. However, in an event such as the Microsoft case, the source is unknown, and the noise source could be anything from intermediate servers in mul-

[45] C. E. Shannon, A Mathematical Theory of Communication, 27 The Bell System Technical Journal (1948).

tiple jurisdictions to encryption or a combination thereof. John Doe suits, though quite common, suffer from a short shelf life since a defendant must be identified in order to be served. This type of event suggests that the noise source consists of multiple intermediate servers, each of which must be sequentially discovered and served with subpoenas. The jurisdictions in which these servers reside each may have separate requirements for discovery. The implications of Shannon inform the courts of the steps that must be taken to trace these intermediate servers and address their local jurisdictional requirements.

2. Rosennean Complexity

Rosen defines complexity: "A system is *simple* if all its models are simulable. A system that is not simple, and that accordingly must have a non-simulable model, is *complex*."[46] While human activity is considered complex, the types of computing systems on the internet are not. However, people operate computer systems and humans perpetrate fraud using them. It follows, therefore, that if we think of a computer fraud as complex, the court's job becomes more difficult. Moreover, because the motivations of various jurisdictions along the path of well-obfuscated fraudulent activity also are the outcomes of human activity, no hard and fast rules for determining jurisdiction will always be adequate. However, by reverting to Shannon and treating each "noise source" uniquely, we may limit or, indeed, eliminate complexity in this case completely.

3. Emergence

The concept of emergence in the social sciences was articulated by Morgan in 1927[47]:

> …the emphasis is not on the unfolding of something already in being but on the outspringing of something that has hitherto not been in being.

This notion has applicability as we endeavor to introduce cyber concepts into the legal system. In fact, the process probably began prior to 1995,

---

[46] Robert Rosen, *Essays on Life Itself* (Columbia University Press, 1 ed. 2000).

[47] Morgan in Geoffrey M. Hodgson, The Concept of Emergence in Social Science: Its History and Importance, 2 Emergence (2000). P66

the date usually quoted as the start of the commercial Internet[48]. It may have begun prior to 1990 when the first commercial ISP went live, and the Internet's predecessor ceased to exist. Emergence – or emergent property – simply is a case where something is introduced into a system for the first time and it evolves to become part of the system. We propose that the concepts in this paper become part of the slowly emerging property of cyber jurisprudence which evolves until it becomes an integral part of the legal system globally. Because the process has begun already, it is for us to assist as the emergence grows and develops until it evolves into that integral part of the system. This approach differs significantly from the extant approach of layering on new cyber laws and concepts. It also is why no new body of law or legal theory needs to be created.

4. Entropy

Information entropy is described in technical detail by Shannon[49]. However, for our purposes we can view it as a measure of randomness. For example, when we analyze malware and see that our sample has a high entropy, we may conjecture that it is encrypted. Likewise, if we have a cyber event that exhibits a high entropy we – referring to Shannon – can conjecture that the noise source is high. Since the legal community is not in the business of Internet traffic data analytics, we may reverse our definition and say that if a Shannon information system has a high noise factor[50], it likely exhibits a high entropy. That has two important implications for the legal community engaged in some form of cyber jurisprudence.

The first implication – the obvious one – is that we are dealing with a very difficult attribution challenge. It is well-recognized that attribution is the most difficult technique challenging Internet scientists and engineers. From a defense perspective this offers "plausible deniability". From the plaintiff perspective it shows clear intent. The second implication is that the legal community, working with the technical community must evolve an approach to identifying and coping with high entropy events. While the Shannon model is important, and, arguably, the most common, there are other examples of high entropy events. Probably the most difficult is dealing with cryptocurrency. Cryptocurrency fraud, theft and theft of resources ("crypto mining") have become a major Internet

[48] William Craig, The History of the Internet in a Nutshell, WebFX, available at https://www.webfx.com/blog/web-design/the-history-of-the-internet-in-a-nutshell/.

[49] See footnote 45

[50] For example, numerous intermediate servers in multiple jurisdictions and, perhaps, encryption, all used as obfuscation techniques.

issue. Understanding the impact of entropy on the practical exercise of cyber jurisprudence poses a significant challenge and one that, when addressed, can offer some practical guidelines for how to handle complicated cases. It is not very different from separating cases into "simple" and "hard". Dworkin defines a hard case as "When a particular lawsuit cannot be brought under a clear rule of law, laid down by some institution in advance...".[51] In difficult cyber-related cases this certainly is an apt description.

VI. The Draft Framework

Noting the four possible Cases in cyberspace above, again we find that only the last one poses any jurisdictional challenge. Experience also teaches that it is the one most likely to be involved with various forms of international cybercrime and the private law consequences of those crimes. In the first case – both parties to a cyber incident reside within the same jurisdiction and the event occurred in that jurisdiction – physical space laws, perhaps with interpretation based upon the definition of cyber science proposed by Stephenson[52], should normally be sufficient. However, there may be cases where a new law or a revision of an existing one may be necessary. This has nothing to do with selecting jurisdiction, although it may be impacted by conflict of laws. In most case, however, personal jurisdiction will be obvious. In the second case – an action begun and ended in a single jurisdiction after passing through another jurisdiction without stopping – jurisdiction issues may be resolved using the laws in place at the time and for the venue involved at start and finish.

The intermediate jurisdiction will not come into play because there is no way to establish minimum contacts when the jurisdiction is, essentially, a piece of wire between the two endpoints. The third case – an action begun in one jurisdiction and ended in another even though passing through a third (or more) without stopping – the jurisdiction issues here are no different than those in the physical space and, as with the second case, there is no substantive contact in the intervening jurisdiction(s). It is the fourth case – an event begun in one jurisdiction and ended in another while passing through, and stopping in, intervening jurisdictions – that poses challenges to internet jurisdiction. A corollary to this is an

51 Ronald Dworkin, Taking Rights Seriously (Bloomsbury Academic. 2013). Chapter 4 "Hard Cases".

52 Peter R. Stephenson, Defining a Cyber Jurisprudence (2017).

event began and ended in the same jurisdiction after passing through, and stopping in, an intervening jurisdiction.

The real challenge here is parsing the resources that are most likely to be universally acceptable on the international stage. From our analysis we find that likely candidates are:

- Place of the harm
- Subsidiarity Principle
- Rule 4 of the First Restatement
- Rules 1, 2 and 3 of the Tallinn Manual
- The Lotus Principle
- Zeran v. America Online
- Zippo Manufacturing Company v. Zippo Dot Com, Inc.

Extracting the aspects of these seven candidates we get a roadmap for starting. The place of the wrong is clear-cut but applies with consistency only in the United States. The subsidiarity principle will apply both in the US and internationally but is not a settled procedure as of this writing. That, however, does not prevent it from being a viable candidate for cyber jurisdiction roadmap.

Rule 4 of the First restatement is useful though somewhat outdated in the US but is useful from perspective of examining fraud (the place of the wrong is where the impact is) and is problematic when looking at the place of the last event necessary to consummate the act (which could be a "zombie[53]" server under no person's direct control). Taken together with the other candidates, it is likely that there will be both US and international usefulness in Rule 4 as guidance. The Tallinn Manual is moderately useful internationally but not as useful within the US. However, the principle that a sovereign entity has control over events and people that are beholden to it or are in jurisdictions that are part of the state. Where its usefulness relative to the United States lies is related to events involving the United States and a foreign state. The Lotus Principle has application internationally and when the US interacts with a foreign State. But within the US it has little value. Zeran v. America Online (AOL) is useful from the perspective that although it dealt with web materials it equally could address other data housed on a server, wherever

[53] "...servers that are physically running but not performing any useful functions." https://www.hpe.com/us/en/insights/articles/your-zombie-server-action-plan-1901.html - zombie servers often are taken over by cyber criminals for use as attack platforms that are difficult to trace to the actor.

that server resides. If the server is a zombie taken over by a hacker, the actual owner of the server could have no liability and, similarly, would not enter a jurisdictional dispute. The principles taught by Zeran could apply to both US and international jurisdictional issues.

Zippo is useful both in the US and internationally for its determination of the role of the principle of minimum contacts. It also indirectly addresses the interests of the forum. The court in Zippo showed that substantive direct contact with the plaintiff's forum allowed personal jurisdiction in that forum. Substantive direct contact is not quite the same as genuine connection which is not universally well-defined.

Taking these elements as applied both in the US and internationally, we get the following link analysis diagram:

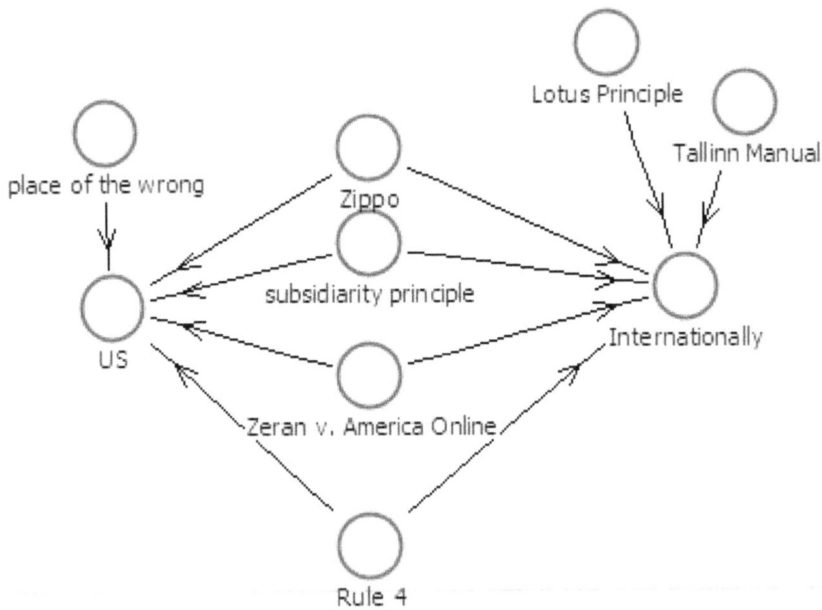

Figure 2 - Mapping of Framework Elements Showing Usefulness in the US and Internationally

As can be seen from the diagram the place of the wrong has affinity with the US but not internationally. Similarly, the Lotus Principle and the Tallinn Manual have affinity internationally but not in the US. However, these affinities are not absolute. Place of the wrong may be recognized under some circumstances internationally.[54] As a starting point, then, we focus on the Zippo case, the subsidiarity principle, the Zeran case and Rule 4 of the First Restatement. We recognize that there will be other elements added as we complete further research, but these four elements provide the starting point for a draft framework. We begin by reiterating the premise that the pedistal upon which our framework will stand is the subsidiarity principle. Even though this is not yet a universally accepted principle, it forms a very good basis for dealing with international incidents in cyberspace where one jurisdiction may be reluctant to pursue the case.

1. The Cyber Jurisdiction Framework

Taking that as a starting point, we establish the first guideline of our framework:

> **Guideline 1** – A State may only exercise its jurisdiction if another State with a purportedly stronger nexus to the case fails to do so in ways that are reasonably acceptable to the would-be regulating State or to the international community at large. States with the strongest nexus to the case forfeit their right of protest against the other States' jurisdictional assertions over that case, if the former States fail to adequately deal with it.[55]
>
> **Guideline 2** – The place of the harm is the place of the impact.
>
> **Guideline 3** – Non-consensual or unauthorized control of Internet or other network-attached devices and computers does not dictate personal jurisdiction in the forum where the devices or computers reside.
>
> **Guideline 4** – Substantive directed contact dictates the jurisdiction unless Rule 3 applies. By "directed" we mean intentional and with knowledge of the contact.
>
> **Guideline 5** – Where settled physical space law exists as to the choice of jurisdiction and the type and nature of anticipated litigation, such as an event that begins and is completed within the same jurisdiction, that law shall be applied, with modifications to address the cyber aspects of the event if necessary. However, simply because an event occurs in

[54] For example, see Regulation (EU) No 1215/2012 of the European Parliament and of the Council of 12 December 2012 (The Brussels Regulation, 2012).

[55] See footnote 27 – the subsidiarity principle.

cyberspace does not indicate that it is a "cyber event" any more than defamation in a newspaper is a "newspaper event".

Guideline 6 – The place of the harm is the first choice for jurisdiction. The forum in the place of the harm may claim personal jurisdiction over other entities involved[56].

Guideline 7 – Where an attack or other wrong acts autonomously, the developer or producer of the offending autonomous code, computer or system is liable. The jurisdiction of the place of the harms may claim personal jurisdiction over that actor.

VII. Conclusions and Future Work

The seven guidelines in the preceding section serve as a starting point for discussion and likely will evolve as discussions and relevant case law – both in the United States and internationally – evolve. However, we address issues in cyber space jurisdiction with a set of guidelines that can help shape jurisdiction determination. These are consistent, though not subservient to, legal norms both in the US and internationally. In 2013, the United Nations made its statement on the applicability of international law in cyberspace.[57] The Report was one of several resulting in a UN resolution in 2018[58]. This conclusion fits well with the seven Guidelines above. However, there still is substantive debate about the relative roles of sovereignty and self-defense in cyberspace. For example, in May 2019, the Attorney General of the UK stated:

> Sovereignty is of course fundamental to the international rules-based system. But I am not persuaded that we can currently extrapolate from that general principle a specific rule or additional prohibition for cyber activity beyond that of a

[56] See footnote 23 – Judge Learned Hand.

[57] "… international law and in particular the United Nations Charter, is applicable and is essential to maintaining peace and stability and promoting an open, secure, peaceful and accessible ICT [Information and Communications Technology] environment." Report of Group of Governmental Experts on Developments in the Field of Information and Telecommunications in the Context of International Security. (2013).

[58] Advancing responsible State behaviour in cyberspace in the context of international security - Resolution adopted by the General Assembly on 22 December 2018 - 73rd session of The United Nations Agenda Item 96 (2018).

> prohibited intervention. **The UK Government's position is therefore that there is no such rule as a matter of current international law**[59]. (emphasis added)

Future work will flesh out this paper with more detail and more examples of references and case law. Particularly, we will focus on the following:

- Testing the Guidelines against actual cases around the world;
- Examining further cases and references for refinements that could be added to the Guidelines;
- Searching for counter-examples where the Guidelines would fail and remediating those points of failure;
- Resolving debates such as the discussion of sovereignty versus self-defense (including, for example, in the area where civil and criminal law converge, "hack-back");
- Building out a more complete model with simple-to-follow flow charts for applying the Guidelines aptly;
- Expanding the example case law and references that can be used by the legal community as examples and cites;
- Expanding the usefulness of Shannon, complexity, entropy and emergence.

References

A Jurisdictional Analysis of Microsoft v. 10 John Does Using IP Address 73.21.204.220. (2018).

Advancing responsible State behaviour in cyberspace in the context of international security - Resolution adopted by the General Assembly on 22 December 2018 - 73rd session of The United Nations Agenda Item 96 (2018).

American Law Institute, Restatement (First) of Conflict of Laws § 377 (American Law Institute. 1934).

American Law Institute, Restatement (Second) of Conflict of Laws § 6 (American Law Institute. 1971).

Bryan A. Garner, *Black's Law Dictionary* (West Publishing Company 6 ed. 1990).

[59] Jeremy Wright, Cyber and International Law in the 21st Century (Speech) (UK Government 2019).

Cedric Ryngaert, *Jurisdiction in International Law* (Oxford University Press. 2008).

C. E. Shannon, *A Mathematical Theory of Communication*, 27 The Bell System Technical Journal (1948).

Dan Jerker B. Svantesson, *Solving the Internet Jurisdiction Puzzle* (Oxford University Press. 2017).

Diana Sancho Villa, *Jurisdiction Over Jurisdiction and Choice of Court Agreements: Views on the Hague Convention of 2005 and Implications for the European Regime*, 12 Yearbook of Private International Law, (2010).

Geoffrey M. Hodgson, *The Concept of Emergence in Social Science: Its History and Importance*, 2 Emergence (2000).

Jack Goldsmith Lea Brilmayer, Erin O'Hara O'Connor, Conflict of Law - Cases and Materials (Wolters Kluwer 7 ed. 2015).

Jeremy Wright, *Cyber and International Law in the 21st Century* (Speech) (UK Government 2019).

Michael N. Schmitt, Tallinn manual 2.0 on the international law applicable to cyber operations (Prepared by the International Groups of Experts at the Invitation of the NATO Cooperative Cyber Defence Centre of Excellence 2 ed. 2017).

Microsoft Corporation v. John Does 1-10 using IP address73.21.204.220, (United States District Court, Western Disctrict of Washington at Seattle).

Peter R. Stephenson, *Defining a Cyber Jurisprudence* (2017).

Peter R. Stephenson, *Jurisdiction in Cyberspace: A Question of Conflict of Laws?* (2018).

Report of Group of Governmental Experts on Developments in the Field of Information and Telecommunications in the Context of International Security. (2013).

Robert Rosen, *Essays on Life Itself* (Columbia University Press 1 ed. 2000).

Ronald Dworkin, *Taking Rights Seriously* (Bloomsbury Academic. 2013).

Unmanned Systems in Homeland Security. (2015).

William Craig, *The History of the Internet in a Nutshell*, WebFX, *available at* https://www.webfx.com/blog/web-design/the-history-of-the-internet-in-a-nutshell/.

Wikipedia, *Lotus Case*, Wikipedia. (2009).

Table of Cases

Reno v. Am. Civil Liberties Union

Zeran v. Am. Online, Inc.
Zippo Mfg. Co. v. Zippo Dot Com, Inc.
ProCD, Inc. v. Zeidenberg
Costar Reality Information Inc. *v.* Field, 737 F. Supp. 2d 496 (D. Maryland 2010)
Religious Tech. Ctr. v. Netcom On-Line Commc'n Servs.
Pres-Kap, Inc. v. Sys. One, Direct Access, Inc.
International Shoe v. State of Washington, 326 U.S. 310 (1945)
Calder v. Jones, 465 U. S. 783 (1984)
Shaffer v. Heitner, 433 U.S. 186 (1977)
S. S. Lotus - France v Turkey
United States v. Aluminum Co. of Am
Barcelona Traction, Light, and Power Company Belgium v Spain
Microsoft Corporation v. John Does 1-10 using IP address 73.21.204.220

CASE NOTE: An Onerous Standard of Care in History Taking (FB v Princess Alexandra Hospital)

Philippa Kemp[1]

Liverpool Law School, School of Law and Social Justice, University of Liverpool.

Summary. In a recent case of appeal against Princess Alexandra Hospital NHS Trust, the Court of Appeal was wrong to find that Dr Rushd breached the standard of care for taking a history in *FB v Princess Alexandra Hospital NHS Trust* [2017] EWCA Civ 334. An analysis of the court's judgment shows that the court has failed to test the standard of care for taking a history against the measure of reasonableness. The application of the measure of reasonableness demonstrates that Dr Rushd did provide a reasonable standard of care. Although the court was right to uphold *Wilsher v Essex AHA* [1987] 1 QB 730 because junior doctors should not be held to a lower standard, this does not justify the Court of Appeal setting the standard of care higher than is expected by a reasonable standard. To uphold this precedent places an onerous burden on GPs.

Introduction

It is submitted that the Court of Appeal's application of the test for breach of duty was flawed in the case of *FB v Princess Alexandra Hospital NHS Trust*.[2] In this case, the child patient FB was examined by the GP Dr Rushd who failed to elicit a key symptom when taking FB's history.

---

[1] Email: pip@kempmail.co.uk.

[2] * Liverpool Law School, School of Law and Social Justice, University of Liverpool.

FB v Princess Alexandra Hospital NHS Trust [2017] EWCA Civ 334; [2017] PIQR P17.

At first instance, the trial judge misapplied the law and dismissed the claim. This was overturned on appeal. In doing so, the Court of Appeal failed to properly consider the reasonableness requirement in determining whether the standard of care had been breached. As such, the standard of care was set higher in this case than it can reasonably be expected from a GP in this context, and so Dr Rushd was found to have breached this standard.

After setting out the facts of the case and the test for negligence, this commentary's analysis of the reasonableness requirement will demonstrate that although high standards of care are expected from medical professionals in the UK, the standard set in this case is unreasonable. Moreover, it is argued that establishing this standard as legal precedent in subsequent case law would place an onerous burden on medical practitioners. It will also be made clear that the care provided by Dr Rushd was both reasonable and dutiful in the context of this case, and thus there was no justifiable reason to elevate the standard of care above the one already provided by Dr Rushd. Finally, this commentary will explore the notion that the responsibility for history taking should be shared by both GP and patient.

Facts

A thirteen-months-old child ("FB") showed signs of ill health from 18th September 2003. On 27th September, FB's mother ("WAC") made three calls to the local out-of-hours service and FB was examined by a GP. FB presented worse symptoms overnight and on the 28th WAC called the local practice again. FB was examined by a second GP Dr Rana during a home visit, who chose not to make a referral. Early morning on the 29th, an ambulance was called by the out-of-hours triage nurse who described FB's condition to the ambulance service as '*temperature …up to 40 she is rolling her eyes and her breathing is a little bit erratic.*'[3] FB arrived at Princess Alexandra Hospital at 4.45am and was examined by Dr Rushd at 5.20am, for approximately 25 minutes, and subsequently 'discharged at 5.55am'.[4] FB's condition deteriorated and later that afternoon she returned to the hospital via ambulance and was immediately referred to paediatrics, thereby examined and administered antibiotics. On 1st October she was transferred to Great Ormond Street Hospital and diagnosed with 'pneumococcal meningitis and multiple brain infarcts'.[5] FB sus-

[3] ibid [8].
[4] ibid [11].
[5] ibid [3].

tained permanent brain damage which resulted in learning difficulties and severe deafness. The parents brought claims in negligence against Dr Rana and against Princess Alexandra Hospital NHS Trust on behalf of Dr Rushd.

Both claims failed at first instance. The trial judge held that neither Dr Rana nor Dr Rushd had breached the required standard of care when conducting their individual examinations of FB and obtaining the patient history. With regards to Dr Rushd's history taking, the claimants alleged that she should have elicited the fact that FB's eyes were rolling when taking the patient's history, a fact which would have led her to make a referral to a paediatrician at the time of examination. The judge held that this did not amount to a breach of duty because only a senior doctor could be expected to procure this information.

On appeal against Princess Alexandra Hospital NHS Trust, the decision regarding Dr Rushd was overturned. The appeal was allowed on the grounds that the trial judge was wrong to conclude that only a 'more senior pair of eyeballs'[6] could be expected to pick up on this symptom, for this contradicts the principle laid down in *Wilsher v Essex AHA*.[7] The Court of Appeal concluded that Dr Rushd could not be held to a lower standard in this case, and by consequence the history taking fell short of the standard of care. The analysis below demonstrates the flawed nature of the court's conclusion.

The Test for Negligence

Within the context of *FB v Princess Alexandra Hospital NHS Trust*,[8] the *Bolam* test[9] for negligence can be applied thus: firstly, that Dr Rushd would be held to the standard of care of a reasonably competent Senior House Officer ("SHO") in an A&E department;[10] and secondly, that Dr Rushd's taking of FB's patient history would not be considered negligent if her actions were accepted by a body of medical opinion[11] capable of withstanding logical analysis.[12]

Regarding the first part of the test, the Court of Appeal's position is not disputed.[13] Following *Wilsher v Essex AHA*, the standard of care is an

---

6 *FB v Rana* [2015] EWHC 1536 (Admin) at [164].
7 *Wilsher v Essex AHA* [1987] 1 QB 730.
8 FB (n1).
9 *Bolam v Friern Hospital and Management Committee* [1957] 1 WLR 582.
10 *FB* (n1) [31] (Thirlwall LJ).
11 *Bolam* (n8) [587] (McNair J).
12 *Bolitho v City and Hackney Health Authority* [1998] AC 232.
13 *FB* (n1) [63] (Jackson J).

objective standard that cannot be reduced on the basis of inexperience and thus, the trial judge indeed erred in finding that a junior doctor would be held to a lower standard of care in taking history.[14]

Yet, the Court of Appeal made comparatively little effort to engage with the second branch of the test. No attempt was made to analyse the reasoning and conclusion of the trial judge that Dr Rushd's examination of FB did not breach the standard of care, nor re-assess the matter on its own merits. This oversight was caused by the court conflating these two matters:

> 'I do not accept the judge's conclusion that only a doctor more senior than Dr Rushd can reasonably have been expected to elicit this important fact. Therefore the judge's decision cannot stand.'[15]

This conflation led to the mistaken conclusion that overturning one conclusion would overturn them both. The two branches of the *Bolam* test must remain distinct and it is grossly insufficient for the court to state that it 'is inevitable' to conclude that Dr Rushd breached the standard of care based purely on the principle in *Wilsher*.

Reasonableness

'The law requires a fair and reasonable standard of care and competence.'[16] In establishing a standard of care, the court should first test it against the measure of reasonableness. Dr Rushd's taking of FB's history could not be characterised as cursory. Her notes were described by the court as 'detailed', the examination lasted 25 minutes, and the diagnosis of an upper respiratory tract infection was deemed 'a common diagnosis in a child of her age in the autumn months'.[17] These facts distinguish the case from those such as *Rhodes v Spokes & Farbridge*,[18] where the notes were poor and the practitioner was not open-minded in his diagnosis; and *Collins v Mid-Western Health Board*,[19] where the doctor asked the patient only one question and did not enquire about the patient's headaches despite having prior knowledge of them. It is submitted

---

[14] *Wilsher* (n6).

[15] FB (n1) [64] (Jackson J).

[16] *R v Bateman* (1927) 19 Cr App R 8 at [12].

[17] *FB* (n1) [16] (Thirlwall J).

[18] *Rhodes v Spokes & Farbridge* [1996] 7 Med LR 135.

[19] *Collins v Mid-Western Health Board and O'Connor* (SC(Irl), 12 November 1999).

that these facts, objectively viewed, could provide an evidential basis for the contention that Dr Rushd demonstrated a reasonable standard of taking history. However, the court was quick to overlook the significance of these facts.

Whilst it was deemed acceptable for Dr Rushd to open with the question 'why are you here' the court criticised her for failing to extend to this to 'why are you here at this time' based on the evidence presented by Dr Evans.[20] It seems arbitrary to assign negligence on the basis of a slight divergence in the wording of a question; not only because it is such a minor point of contention, but also because there is no regulatory guidance for doctors for history taking.[21] It must be acknowledged that a lack of official guidance was held not to be determinative in excusing negligence where a range of evidence can be consulted to determine whether there was an established practice.[22] However, this only serves to signify that the court should consider expert evidence in more depth in this regard. In *Burne v A*[23] it was held that the use of open questions by a GP during a telephone interview with the patient child's mother was reasonable, and as Carson and Shawyer elucidate it 'was inappropriate to find the doctor negligent when his actions had been consistent with professional practice' in this case.[24] It can therefore be argued that the court should not dismiss evidence in defence of Dr Rushd's actions lightly, because although the court may be entitled to say that a particular approach is appropriate or even required in a certain context, retrospectively dictating the phrasing or precise detail of questions places an onerous burden on doctors which they cannot hope to fulfil, particularly in the absence of any official guidance. That is not to say that medical practice guidelines should not exist; only that it is not the courts' role to dictate it.

The submissions of Dr Evans were rejected by the trial judge because they had 'a tendency towards circularity, and to rely on hindsight',[25] supporting the notion that the standard they advocate is unrealistic and thus too high. The Court of Appeal discredited the trial judge's argument on the premise that 'the fact that there is no clear precipitating factor in many cases is not an answer to a failure to elicit such a factor when there is one,' [26] and thus concurred with Dr Evans' belief that that Dr Rushd breached the standard of care by not eliciting the fact that FB's eyes were

[20] *FB* (n1)[16], [33] & [47] (Thirlwall J).

[21] ibid [43] (Thirlwall J).

[22] *Sullivan v Guy's and St Thomas' NHS Foundation Trust* [2017] EWHC 602 (QB); [2017] Med LR 260.

[23] *Burne v A* [2006] EWCA Civ 24; [2006] All ER 172.

[24] David Carson and Andrea Shawyer, 'Interviewing conundrums' [2006] 156 NLJ 1515.

[25] *FB v Rana* (n5) [168].

[26] FB (n1) [43] (Thirlwall J).

rolling. It is surprising that the Court of Appeal was so quick to dismiss the analysis of the expert evidence by the trial judge, and yet the court itself neglected to review the expert evidence in its judgment. If the court wished to override the trial court and instead accept the evidence presented by Dr Evans, the principle laid down in *Bolitho v City and Hackney HA* dictates that this evidence must first be 'capable of withstanding logical analysis' by the court.[27] The Court of Appeal's judgement refers to Dr Evan's evidence concurring with its own conclusions such as that 'in those circumstances it might be thought obvious to seek to establish what had caused the parents to bring her to hospital in the early hours'. Yet in the absence of any logical analysis of Dr Evans' submissions, this expert evidence fails to provide convincing support for the court's conclusions.

In addition, the trial judge acknowledged that a doctor 'cannot know the number of occasions on which patients, for whatever reason, have omitted to give a full history.'[28] This is not, as the Court of Appeal surmised, 'an approach predicated on a mistaken belief that there are some things that do not need to be asked about'.[29] Instead, it is an acknowledgement that a doctor's power of questioning has its limits. Where a doctor is not omniscient, they cannot be expected to continue arbitrarily questioning a patient for an inordinate length of time to fully satisfy their curiosity and ensure they have obtained every facet of information about the patient's health, character, and ipseity. While this is an extreme interpretation of what an inexhaustible standard for history taking may require, it serves to demonstrate the need for upholding and not exceeding a reasonable standard of care for history taking.

Shared Responsibility

There is also an argument to be made that the patient should share the responsibility of history taking. Brodie and Mason argue that the *Bolam* test is flawed because it takes no account of patient autonomy.[30] As the influence of patient autonomy in medical care continues to grow,[31] we must also question the extent of patient responsibility. Draper and Sorell make a convincing argument that 'autonomous patients do have duties' in

---

[27] *Bolitho* (n11) [243] (Lord Browne-Wilkinson).

[28] *FB v Rana* (n5) [89].

[29] *FB* (n1) [41] (Thirlwall J).

[30] Douglas Brodie and Kenyon Mason, 'Bolam, Bolam - wherefore are thou Bolam?' [2005] 9 Edin LR 298.

[31] Margaret Brazier, 'Patient autonomy and consent to treatment: the role of the law?' [1987] 7 Legal Studies 169.

their medical care which are 'left out of mainstream medical ethics'.[32] In particular, they highlight that the 'main duty of patients' is 'co-operating with doctors'.[33] Brazier concurs, recognising the 'moral responsibilities' of patients.[34] Although proper analysis of this is beyond the scope of this comment, surely the duty of the parents to co-operate with medical professionals on behalf of the child patient FB should be held to an equal, or even higher, standard than the duty of an autonomous patient. It is interesting to note that the Court of Appeal took the position that the symptom of FB's eyes rolling was the obvious precipitating factor in this case, and yet did not justify why the blame for the symptom not being disclosed fell solely on Dr Rushd. If it were so obvious, it begs the question why the parents, the only witnesses of the symptom, did not volunteer the information to the doctor. This is especially poignant considering that this symptom was previously disclosed by WAC to a nurse and paramedics, yet was never mentioned during the examination by Dr Rushd.[35]

Conclusion

This comment has established that Dr Rushd's history taking in this case has held up against the measure of reasonableness and has met the required standard of care. Furthermore, the conclusion of the Court of Appeal is based on flawed reasoning and an incorrect application of the law. The standard of care applied in this case is clearly arbitrary and cannot be borne. The courts cannot and should not seek to place additional burden on the medical profession by imposing elevated standards of care without due justification.

---

32 Heather Draper and Tom Sorell, 'Patients' Responsibilities in Medical Ethics' [2002] 16 Bioethics 335, 350.

33 ibid 352.

34 Margaret Brazier, 'Do no harm – do patients have responsibilities too?' [2006] 65 CLJ 397, 422.

35 *FB* (n1) [9].

BOOK REVIEW: Research Handbook on Copyright

Review by David Felipe Alvarez Amezquita[1]

University of Tolima, Colombia

Paul Torremans, ed. *Research Handbook on Copyright Law.* Second Edition. Research Handbooks in Intellectual Property series. Edward Elgar Publishing, 2017. ISBN 978 1 78536 142 5. 624pp.

Introduction

Copyright clearly faces the constant challenge of achieving a balance between confluent interests of several stakeholders. As it is an area of the law related to culture and science, it touches multiple aspects of legal analysis from philosophy, international law to criminal and private law. This Research Handbook on Copyright presents questions and challenges on copyright issues that project the discipline in the future. This book offers a broad perspective of areas to consider of possible research about copyright. Although most of the attention is paid to issues related to EU copyright law and its problems of harmonisation, it also reflects global issues and interesting perspectives from other jurisdictions.

Contents

The first chapter on the book proposes the metaphor of the tightrope to show the efforts that copyright faces towards achieving a balance between stakeholders. Such a metaphor could represent a good resume of the general idea the whole book shows. The constant tension to achieve a balance indicates that copyright has opened its ears to understand not only the interests of the rightsholders, but also the interests of the users and other persons or entities engaged in one or another form with copyright.

While it is difficult to reduce into a short space the wide variety of issues considered by the authors selected in this book, it is proposed here

[1] Email: dfalvareza@gmail.com

to group some of the chapters in to two main bundles of works, those related to EU issues and those not directly related to such issues. Nevertheless, the two first chapters will have first attention, separated from the two proposed bundles, as these two offer important reflexions towards the research on copyright in terms of the connecting points of the debates found along the book and the role of history in the comprehension of such problems.

The balance conundrum

The first chapter on the book is titled "Walking the Copyright Tightrope". Gendreau's text highlights the major issue concerning the discipline: the difficult balance between proprietary interests and user's interests. Her metaphor she proposes is useful as it surpasses the usual symbol of a scale by telling us that the balance conundrum for copyright moves, it walks on a tightrope, meaning it has to both adapt to a changing reality and achieve balance at each step.

Of those steps, the author focuses her attention on some of the tensions that Canadian copyright development shows. Such an approach has let the author identify possible sources of stress in the rope. Gendreau suggests that some of those tensions can be visible and some others can be found hidden.

The author then analyses those visible tensions. One of which is between the scope of the economic rights and a 'para-copyright' established as a tool to protect the mechanisms developed to control the use of copyrighted work or the management of such uses. The author questions to what extent such a 'para-copyright' stresses the very nature of copyright. Another of the issues in the visible tensions for copyright is its relationship with the neighbouring rights. This might be a consequence of the tension that Canadian copyright law might have between the common law tradition of copyright and the continental tradition of a 'French' *droit d'auteur*. The tension Gendrau attempts to highlight there, is that related to a possible or not hierarchy between these two types of rights, characterised by their different nature, origin and historical treatment both nationally and internationally.

Other visible tensions are perhaps more traditional as such. Moral rights in the hands of authors can be a nightmare for the copyright owners of the economic right to the extent of author's 'inclination towards unreasonableness'. Copyright's exceptions are a constant source of tension with the economic rights. In every step on the rope, copyright must manage itself to satisfy both interests. As technology pushes one step, the balance changes and copyright has to be reassessed and react. In no few cases, such reassessment implies not only modifying copyright but also questioning its very core. Is the creation of remuneration rights undermining the exclusive rights that have been identified as a core element of copyright? Are those the result of exceptions to copyright or a new mechanism to guarantee rightsholders income? Finally, under the scope of the visible tensions, there are the tensions related to collective societies. On one hand the tension that creates the appearance of different cross-linking situations in which some collective societies might cannibalise other sister organisations, and also, and in my opinion a really important issue, often forgotten in the copyright equation, which is the role of artist's association in the negotiation of contractual relationships between authors and producers of any kind.

The balance conundrum creates, according to Gendrau, some hidden tensions as well. Those tensions, related to what justifies copyright, indicate the usual possibilities in understanding this field. Is it possible to accept that it is a property, even if there are some prerogatives which are not exactly fit the traditional concept of property, as in the case of moral rights? Or is it a tool to regulate economic situations and interests? Neither of those possibilities is absolute. Gendrau highlights that, as an economic regulator copyright is able to respond to the constant change that the development of new forms of use present. Either way, the hidden tensions are related to stakeholders, and often they can shift in the role they play in the complex net of relations between authors, producers, other authors, the public in general, employer or commissioning parties. Often, however, such tensions have been identified under the basis of an individualistic approach to the discipline, and Gendrau attracts the idea to question if is it time to reconsider other collective identities as player in the game, not only the traditional ones such as the collective societies. In the same token, new phenomenon such a social media and the transformation of how works are experienced determines cases in which mass behaviour affects copyright.

On the history of copyright

In this second chapter, Tawfik highlights the interconnections that understanding the development of copyright has with cultural history and book history. The author uses Robert Darnton's proposal on the communication circuit which begins with the writers, to the publisher and all that is needed for the publication of the book, towards the reader who could be finally another author. As Tawfik indicates, copyright history cannot be separated from the cultural history, but it cannot use book history as a mere tool supporting contemporary policies for the discipline either. The interactions between both areas of knowledge are deeper and deserve more attention. The author in this chapter explores how history studies (particularly those related to book history, and cultural history we must add) can help in understanding copyright policies, and for this purpose, three common law countries (the UK, the US and Australia) were studied.

By using Tawfik's considerations on a broader perspective, some new understandings would emerge from connecting copyright development in the twentieth century with the cultural histories of countries that arrived at the international arena later in the middle of the century. That is the case of most of the African countries and some of the Latin American countries. As Tawfik asserts, '(t)he narratives of those who directly or indirectly accessed the copyright system or who were agents of change within the system or who were especially affected offer a more robust appreciation of copyright law in action.'[2] Some questions loom, though. What is the influence of more recent developments in both areas, the contemporary histories of copyright and the book? The twentieth century walked copyright towards its unification and globalisation through the consolidation of the Berne Convention as one of the most broadly extended IP treaty (to the date 185 members are part of the 1971 Paris Act). What is the role of other countries beyond Europe and the north of America in such a development? Is it possible to ask similar questions to other times and other jurisdictions? Nevertheless, this chapter shows a very important attempt of calling the attention of both historians and lawyers to produce interdisciplinary studies in which they can interact.

The harmonisation problems

Originality in the pitch of harmonisation of EU copyright law

From a thorough study of the CJEU´s case law, Stamatoudi reaches some conclusions in relation to the problem of define the concept of originality for copyright as the primary requirement to provide its protection to a work. It is clear for the author that there is a tendency in the case law to harmonise such a concept, even if there is not a general definition of it in the EU Directives on copyright. The case law shows that the basic criterion is that the work should display the expression of author´s intellectual creation. The problem is how to adapt such criterion in the relevant national context, particularly in the case of the UK and its own tradition based on common law. While civil law has higher standards of originality, the UK has different ones, particularly in the case of requiring just skill and labour and requiring the fixation of the work. Nevertheless, in the case of the European countries, it is also important to accept that there shouldn't be any distinction regarding the nature of the work in or-

[2] Myra J Tawfik, 'Copyright History as Book History: The Law Inmultidisciplinary Context' in Paul Torremans (ed), *Research Handbook on Copyright Law* (2nd edn, Edward Elgar Publishing 2017). 34.

der to apply the originality criterion. The author also explored the scope of originality in the case of computer programs, in which case the protection is related to the program itself. Other elements, those that if reproduced they would not require the reproduction of the software or part of it, would not constitute original parts of the software, whilst they might consist in an independent original work. Two main conclusions are presented by Stamatoudi. One is that the originality criterion in the continent is higher than in those countries based on the common law, and two, that a distinctive criterion for different types of work is not applicable under EU law.

The exclusive rights in the EU's landscape. Attention to the communication to the public

In his chapter, Torremans explores the case law of the CJEU related to the right of communication to the public. This right enables the rightsholder to control the access to the work by members of the public gathered or not at the same place. This is a zoom out view of a problem highlighted by the author, which is that the EU Directives on copyright have left open spaces on defining the scope of the exclusive rights conceded to the author. The case of communication to the public is relevant, as the number of articles related to this subject within the book shows. In Torremans' chapter, the problems related to hyperlinks are studied. In the author´s opinion, based on the study of the case law, there is a difference between deep linking and mere hyperlink as in the latter, the intervention of the linker is less prominent than the intervention of the deep linker. There are also the implications of this problem regarding the protection of other rights involved, as in the case of freedom of expression. Whether it is required to limit restrictions to these rights in the case of communication to the public or not, would be a matter of case by case study. Torremans suggests that the nature of the user, whether it is a non-for-profit entity or a commercial one, should alter the result in the analysis. The non-profit user would imply less ability to be aware of the eventual illegality of the source, instead, a commercial user would probably well aware of such a risk.

Brison & Depreeuw analyse the problem expanding the point of view by focusing also in the case law of the CJEU, but including the view towards the international level. With such an expansion, the authors suggest that there has been a movement en route to an abstract concept of communication rather than specialised rights for different types of acts. However, the authors also suggest, the criteria for such an abstract concept of communication to the public, as it has been developed by the CJEU's case law need to be weighted in order to provide guidance. Whether the criterion is that there are different technical mechanisms allowing the communication, or that the communicator has reached a new public (different from the initially intended by the authorised use), or if there should be knowledge of the legality of the communication, or if interest in profit commands the use, the CJEU is in due time to provide some guidance regarding these criteria.

Gaetano Dimita explores the right to make the work available to the public. This right comes from what it has been called the "umbrella solution" established by the WIPO Copyright Treaty (WCT) of 1996. Such an umbrella solution, the consequence of the difficulties within WIPO of defining thoroughly the internet uses that would be subject to control by the copyright owner, left open many questions as it has been highlighted by the author in this chapter. Those questions are, as Dimitia suggests: the relation of this right with other rights (reproduction, broadcasting, distribution and public performance), as well as the activities that might constitute making available to the public, who does it, where and when. The consequence explored by this author regards how the provision established by article 8 of the WCT has been implemented. For this purpose, and after describing the WIPO treaties, the author compares the EU and the US implementations of this right. On one hand, the EU has adopted a similar language to introduce the umbrella solution through the Directive 2001/29/EC, opening the possibility to several decisions from the CJEU on the matter as it has been explored in the previous chapters. On the other hand, the US has not changed its legislation on the matter of making available the work to the public. To complete a broader view, the author also indicates, with less attention how other jurisdictions, such as Australia, China, Canada and Japan, have implemented the right on comment.

Dimitia's conclusions are that the umbrella solution has created uncertainties that have not been cleared after 20 years of creation of the figure. The balance conundrum has been shown here as one of the problems the interpretation of the right of making available has created, as the author indicates that judges tend to expand the concept as much as possible in order to protect author's interests. The author also highlights some common concerns regarding the problems of knowledge, intent and intervention which shown in the EU and the US case law about this right. In his opinion, those concerns should lead in achieving the desired balance.

From the EU perspective, regarding the right of communication to the public, Justin Koo proposes an interesting element referred to the jurisdiction problems that this right represents. Given that the protection of copyright remains fundamentally territorial, the author suggests that in case of ubiquitous infringement and in order to improve the enforcement of the right, the legislation should clarify that 'the act of communication to the public occurs in the country(ies) of reception and that the person responsible for that act is the one who actively initiated the 'communication'.'[3]

Towards European moral rights

Another of the issues worked in this book in relation to the harmonisation difficulties of the EU Law on copyright is the protection of moral rights. Janssens indicates that the lack of case law on the matter within the decisions of the CJEU is the result of its non-regulation in the EU Directives. While it has been admitted that moral rights are important within the EU context, even more in the case of the digital environment, the arduous process to conciliate the difference among the country members, has implied that this issue has been left aside in the directives. The author explores some of the problems such a process would face, for instance, the traditional clash between common law and civil law approaches, but nevertheless, also the problems that implementing moral rights might create for freedom of contract, and the question of whether the EU is competent in regulating such a matter. The author of this chapter invites to study possible ways to include moral rights within the EU copyright law. One of the main points to study is to establish whether the interests that are meant to be protected by moral rights are any longer of the interest of society. A tough question, I think, but an important one as it is relevant for the whole system if the protection of authorship and its relationship with creativity and art, are still important issues to ultimately protect. In addition, it would be required to identify the floor to which the protection of moral rights might need to reach. For instance, are those rights definitively not to be waived? Should these rights be subject to a term of protection? To what extent those rights should exist? Can these rights be subjected by limitations or exceptions?

The resale right and the collective management in the EU Law

This chapter analyses if mandatory collective management is the only possible solution for achieving the resale right objective, which is that the authors must enjoy a share in the economic success of their works of art. The study explores how three European countries, the Netherlands, Belgium, and France have implemented the resale right with or without compulsory collective management. The harmonisation of this right did not regulate this matter, leaving the countries free to decide the model by which the right would be exercised. The conclusions the author offers is that there is no need to oblige the country members to create compulsory

[3] Justin Koo, 'Enforcing the EU Right of Communication to the Public in Cases of Ubiquitous Infringement' in Paul Torremans (ed), *Research Handbook on Copyright Law* (1st edn, Edward Elgar Publishing 2017). 199.

management as it has been shown that the either possibilities are able to achieve the goal proposed by the EU Directive 2001/84/EC.

Limits to freedom of contract to favour author's rights

Agnès Lucas-Schloetter opens the debate to of freedom of contract in copyright law. Supported in Dietz, this author recognises that copyright contract law is one of the five pillars for the modern discipline. The problem regarding this issue is that the continental countries have a stronger legislation towards the protection of author's and performers' remuneration. The issue at stake is to what extent freedom of contract must be limited to protect such a remuneration. If one of copyright's aims is to guarantee a reward for the creative people, the imbalance in the bargain position between authors and producers has to be solved by the law. The author highlights how in the European context, most of the countries have regulations created in order to restore such an imbalance. This has been achieved either through ex-ante mechanisms or ex-post mechanisms. In the first case those mechanisms are aimed to guarantee through the contract an adequate remuneration to the author. In the second case, the mechanisms respond to how the contract and the work have performed. Therefore, some clauses such as the best seller clause are meant to improve author's revenues in case of disproportionate remuneration. The same end operates in the case of termination of the contract and the possibility of revert the rights to their original owner. The mechanism operates through periodic revisions of the contract development in order to modify its conditions if the market changes, or the implementation of limitations in the duration of the contract by which after certain time the author and the producer would need to renegotiate. This chapter is linked clearly, although not mentioned, to the EU proposal for fair remuneration for authors within the proposed Directive on copyright in the digital single market. It highlights that in the European context there are more possibilities than the ex-post mechanism proposed for the mentioned directive, indicating that this is a clear characteristic of continental countries which accept that there is not possible to claim freedom of contract when there is a difference in the bargain power among the parties in the contractual relationship.

Exclusion of copyright based on morality or public policies

For the sake of the discussion, the possibility of creating an exclusion for copyright, similar to the exclusions that exist for inventions in the field of industrial property, is an interesting topic. However, I cannot agree with such an idea as a matter of principle. Excluding copyright material from protection based upon moral or public policies reasons seems awfully close to censorship, even if it is the case of content in which something unacceptable is mentioned or indicated. The author has given some examples of cases in which such exclusion may apply. From films related to the sexual exploitation of children to women wearing burkinis at the beach. The moral maze that our society faces cannot be solved through copyright exclusions. The main purpose of copyright is precisely the opposite, promoting freedom of expression by giving equal proprietary rights to authors who have created original works. Every work has the same rights, and each of them competes in the market of knowledge and it is a matter for the audience whether to prefer Bukowski over Goebbels. If history has taught us a lesson, is that by censoring materials is the best way to promote them, and by excluding of copyright protection certain works would create the effect that such a work would be in the public domain, free from proprietary restrictions. All the opposite of what the author of this chapter seeks. But what does this author seek? Pila indicates that the aim of this chapter is to search for an objective justification for the exclusion. The main argument supporting the idea is the protection of fundamental rights within the EU framework.

I will take one of the examples the author uses in order to support this idea. The *Deckmyn v. Vandersteen* case shows a problem regarding the allowed use of the parody exception (Article 5(3)(k) of Directive 2001/29) in a depiction of an existing work. In the case, the depiction of the original work changes some of its items. For the Court, the parody exception has to strike a balance between the interests of the person who used the original work in a free manner and the interests of the author of the original work. If the parody use somehow affects the original work by associating it with derogative conveyed images (for instance, in the case, a discriminatory message), the required balance might not be achieved as the secondary use affects directly the interest of the author of the original work. However, by no means, such a ruling implies that a derogative message by itself should not deserve copyright protection (if original). The ruling intends it to protect the original work by not allowing that a derogative massage not intended by the original author might be associated with that work by the means of a parody. The author of this chapter stresses the ruling to a point not indicated in the Court's decision: '…any subject matter capable of conveying a message of discrimination – such as an image of veiled people of colour collecting coins from the street – might be inappropriate for copyright and related rights protection on the basis of the Charter's prohibition against discrimination'[4]. One might not agree with the ruling either, as if the parody can effectively be

[4] Justine Pila, 'Copyright and Related Rights: Outlining a Case for European Morality/Public Policy Exclusion' in Paul Torremans (ed), *Research Handbook on Copyright Law* (1st edn, Edward Elgar Publishing 2017). 450-451.

separated from the original work in a manner that no confusion can be created in the audience, no restriction should be applied to limit user's freedom of expression protected through the parody exception. Nevertheless, the Court's ruling does not go where Pila pretends, it just tries to achieve a level of protection that would not affect the author's reputation.

Although this is taking more space than the used for other chapters, I think it is important to analyse further the elements of discussion the author presents. For instance, by studying the case law related to the exclusions for patents and trade marks, the author infers that similar arguments can be applicable to copyright. But that might not be the case. Whilst in the case of trade marks and patents, the property rights are balanced against morality and public policy, in the case of copyright is freedom of expression what it is at stake. For instance, while denying protection to a trade mark that affects morality or public policies would achieve the protection of such interests, two possible effects might have to deny protection to a work contrary to the morality or public policies. Either the work will be made free of access, or, if what Pila pretends is achieved, it would impede that others have the opportunity to rebuke the morally un acceptable work. I am not supporting here that any work should circulate freely in the market, it is clear that certain works should need some control in order to protect certain members of the public characterised by their vulnerability, but that is not the purpose or the task of copyright. It is also not enough supported that by excluding a work of copyright protection, its dissemination will be reduced. Clearly, the incentive copyright promotes would not be there, but by no means, this will impede the work to be disseminated, particularly in a digital environment in which self-publication is just some clicks away. Even worse if, as the author proposes, any relief for the infringement of the denied rights, should also be banned. Therefore, no discouraging means whatsoever regarding the illegal dissemination of work could be possible from the point of copyright.

The author of this chapter concludes proposing two principles for the creation of exclusions for copyright based on morality or public policies grounds. The principles are meant to open the margin of decision of the countries to determine the grounds based on morality or public policy to denied copyright protection, either based on the national requirements of public policies or EU policies protecting fundamental interests.

EU private international law and copyright

Torremans develops this last chapter analysing how the EU international private law framework copes with the challenges that represent the possible cross-border infringements of copyright and the cross-border licensing issues on copyright. While it is not a matter of harmonisation itself, the chapter clearly points towards that direction as part of the analysis suggested depends on the level of harmonisation of copyright law in the

EU. His work starts from the premise that there is not an international copyright law, but different national systems that follow the parameters of international regulations establishing standards of minimal protection. Within the EU framework, the Brussels I Regulation is the legal basis for the analysis. The author uses a typical case of internet infringement of copyright to indicate the possible issues of international law that may occur. One is the possibility of following the principle of established on article 4 of the Brussels I Regulation by which prosecution would be initiated in the country of the defendant. Nevertheless, such a principle is not suitable for more complex cases in which, as Torremans suggests, for instance the defendant did not commit any infringement in the forum, or it is situated far away from the country where the rightsholder is based, or there are multiple defendants. In such cases other regulation may come to hand.

Torremans suggests that article 7(2) could help on the issue, as it establishes that the jurisdiction may apply following the place where the harmful actions have occurred and the place of the damage. After studying the application of this regulation to copyright cases, the author suggests the importance of tuning the interpretation of such rule in order to help its application for copyright cases. A tool suggested in this chapter is the proviso the European Max Plank Group on Conflicts of Laws in Intellectual Property has proposed for infringement cases (article 2:202). According to the author, the proviso creates a filter by which the infringer cannot be sued in a State in which he/she has not acted "to initiate or further the infringement and her/his activity cannot reasonably be seen as having been directed to that State."[5] Nevertheless, the proviso helps for some cases but does not for those cases of ubiquitous infringement, in which the 7(2) rule would imply that the rightsholder should sue on a country-by-country basis. In such cases, the CLIP principles cited above propose another proviso (article 2:203) under which it would be possible to extend the jurisdiction for copyright cases, as indicated in the 2:202 proviso. Such an extension of the jurisdiction would apply to infringements that occurred or may occur in another State.

In the case of multiple defendants, the author suggests that article 8(1) of the Brussels I Regulation can be applied as it is possible to assert in some copyright cases that the right infringed is a single right. Torremans criticises the Roche case and the theory of the spider in the web developed by the Dutch courts. This because what article 8(1) requires is not a

[5] European Max Planck Group on Conflict of Laws in Intellectual Property. Conflict of Law in Intellectual Property: The CLIP Principles and Commentary (Oxford University Press, 2013), 69. Cited by Paul Torremans, 'Copyright Jurisdiction under EU Private International Law' in Paul Torremans (ed), *Research Handbook on Copyright Law* (1st edn, Edward Elgar Publishing 2017). 565.

link between the claims to be initiated in each country, but that the risk of irreconcilable judgements as a result of separated proceedings is present.

Torremans conclusions are that within the EU framework of private international law there is room for improvement regarding litigation in intellectual property matters.

Other issues

Sampling in Germany or sampling in the US

Sampling implies legal questions that have been responded differently depending on the jurisdictions where the protection is sought. Justin Jütte proposes a revision on how the case law in Germany and in the US have developed the possibility of sampling. One of the most interesting areas the author explores is the interaction of the proprietary rights and the protection of freedom of creativity when considering sampling as a form of art. From a human rights perspective, Jütte indicates that in absence of limitation or exceptions protecting the sampling activity, it might be useful to consider the protection of fundamental rights. A question of balance rises again in this case, between such a fundamental right and the property rights. According to this author, this is an important line of work for the future interpretation regarding the sampling activity. For the author, within the jurisdictions studied, there are not conclusive decisions on the legality of sampling. In the US, the Supreme Court is in due time to solve the problem applying the de minimis approach, which indicates that if the audience can recognise the part of the music used in the new creation, the threshold has been reached and there would be an infringement. However, the author explains the nature of the split that the Supreme Court must solve. Another case had rejected the *de minimis* approach under the argument that such an exception does not apply for sound recordings. In Germany, the scope of the free use exception is not sufficient for samples of longer extension, unless the sample is covered by the concept of artistic uses case in which the protection of fundamental rights might play an important role for its legal use. The other option at hand is the parody exception, but in this case, the interpretation of the CJEU is narrow, giving less space for the sampling activity. Nevertheless, the author suggests that it is now for the EU to define how to deal with the sampling activity.

Portability

Another of the major problems copyright faces in the EU context, and around the globe, is the possibility of accessing internet services such as Netflix in cross-border situations. The problem is related to the territorial nature of copyright and the traditional control that producers create to divide markets. However, such a division, associated to the distribution right might not be useful in the case of streaming services. In their chapter, Riis & Schovsbo suggest that through competition law it is possible to reduce the problems that portability represent, and that there is no need to modernise copyright law on this matter. According to these authors, the agreements restricting the access for the end-user to works through online services from one country to another might be in violation of articles 102 (restrain to competition) and 101 (abuse of a dominant position) TFEU. In the authors opinion, competition law might offer proper tools in which it has to be considered not only the interests of the users but also the legitimate interests of the rightsholders to obtain an appropriate remuneration. Balance is then the magic work again: 'maximising overall social benefits and not special interest groups, be that cross-border users or copyright holders. Competition law analyses are, in fact, rather apt for doing so.'[6] Nevertheless, the authors remind us, while agreements in which territorial delineation is established might be void if they are contrary to competition rules, the existing copyright on the contents implicates that there would be an infringement if the user accesses the content through the service provider in a country in which the provider does not hold the right to do it so.

Private copying

The balancing conundrum can be also identified in Minero's chapter on the private copy. The question the author discusses relates to the nature of the payments that the exception requires as to compensate the holders of the copyright implicated. In her chapter, she focuses on the Spanish experience on private copying and how the model of compensation operates. Very interesting is the decision of the Court of Justice regarding the State's financing the compensation due for the private copying. In the consideration of the Court, this is not acceptable within the InfoSoc Directive. The answer indicates that the State should not be responsible for paying such a levy as it is in its nature that the one that has caused the harm should compensate it. In addition, the Court indicates also that the private copying exception is related to natural persons and not to legal persons, whom cannot be authorised by the exception to freely copy protected works. In such a case, compensation is not in order but prior authorisation and payment.

---

[6] Thomas Riis and Jens Schovsbo, 'The Borderless Online User: Carving up the Market for Online and Streaming Services' in Paul Torremans (ed), *Research Handbook on Copyright Law* (1st edn, Edward Elgar Publishing 2017). 317.

Spanish copyright ownership for researchers

Transfer of knowledge has been an important issue for research institutions and universities around the world. The Spanish perspective, from the point of view of the author of chapter 14, might be unique within the EU, as it regulates the transfer of ownership for works created by researcher through the copyright laws. Cámara Águila studies the sequence of reforms implemented in Spain towards the improvement of this country's structure for the transfer of knowledge. In her conclusion, the special treatment the law has created for the activities of Spanish researchers the general rule of ownership of the works created in the authors' hands. Nevertheless, this author indicates, the research centres and Universities can be entitled as derivative owners, either through the general rules of transference or in the case of collective works, to those rights they require for the purpose of their activities.

Orphans

Within the balance conundrum the problem of the so-called orphan works tells us about a new race, the one for cultural access. Suthersanen suggests that such a race has been ran differently in the US and in Europe. After indicating the known causes for this race on the tightrope, the implications that the digital age has on new ways of creativity and new ways of dissemination, the extension of the term of protection (particularly in the US), the multiple and confusing permissions that might be required for the use of a given work, the automatic protection change which in the US implied an dramatic reduction of the public domain, the author describes the general issues about orphan works and compares some of the systems that have implemented this matter in the US, with special attention to the Google case, the EU, and the French approach. The author also studies two possibilities within the scope of action of the collective management societies (CMOs), one is using blanket licenses in which case there is a problem regarding the absence of mandate in the case of orphan works, and the other is the extended collective licensing in which the law extends the CMO's mandate to non-members authors in order to guarantee full coverage of the repertoires. After this study, Suthersanen comments on the consequences of the cooperation between cultural and heritage institutions and tech companies and the interest of these last in maintaining some proprietary rights in some of the results of such cooperation schemes. The problem there, according to this author, is related to other rights involved such as the rights of authors or the rights of indigenous peoples on their traditional cultural expressions. The new uses of digitalised materials under the umbrella of cultural and heritage institutions, might not be in the scope or the purpose of the race for cultural access. Even more in cases in which the institution withholding the cultural expression belongs to one jurisdiction and the expression itself is from another.

Intangible cultural heritage and freedom of expression

Charlotte Waelde's chapter inspires interesting questions for copyright and its interaction with the protection of intangible cultural heritage (ICH). Her analysis indicates copyright's necessary involvement with contemporary ICH. New expressions and the entanglement of traditional expressions in new forms of appropriation necessarily imply the dawn of new copyright ownerships. The author highlights some issues to consider regarding this matter. For instance, the ICH has been considered as part of the public domain, but this is not necessarily the case and certainly not in the case of living ICH in which the rights of creators might be involved. Nevertheless, says Waelde, as it struggles with the concept of group or collective authorship, copyright law often does not offer ways matching the nature of such creations. Such a struggle creates problems regarding the ownership of those creations of contemporary ICH, leaving them vulnerable. In addition, some other issues create concerns. That is the case of the inventories required for the preservation of such ICH which might be passive of misappropriation. Also creates concerns the interaction between ICH and the protection of freedom of expression. From the copyright perspective, it is indicated that freedom of expression is protected through two basic principles, the idea-expression dichotomy and the limitations and exceptions to copyright. Consequently, Waelde highlights three elements that come to the discussion, ICH-related law, copyright law, and human rights law. According to this author, when copyright is considered as a tool to promote the cultural rights, 'rather than being a tool of commodification, copyright becomes a means for the realisation of the (human rights) goals of cultural rights and of the right to culture, of which ICH is a part'. What the challenges are? Copyright must structure its limitations and exceptions in a way in which contemporary ICH can fulfil its purpose, which means some uses must be accepted whilst other such as the commercial ones will need to be under the control provided by copyright.

Search engines

Ernesto Rengifo analyses the implications of using parts of works by search engines, as in the case of snippets or other uses related to the activity of those systems. The question that the author presents is related to whether those uses are or must be under the scope of protection of copyright or should be considered as part of limitations or exceptions required for the very functioning of the Internet. Rengifo compares the possible mechanisms the law from the US, the EU and the Andean Community have that might apply to the problem. His conclusion regards the analysis of the scope of decision that judges have to determine if such uses are under an exception to copyright or not. The fair use doctrine seems to respond to the interest of promoting creativity, opening the scope of interpretation of the judge to assess whether the use benefits such a principle. For instance, the author highlights, in the case of snippets the fair use doctrine served the purpose of accessibility to the public of parts of works and as the parts are shown are not substantial ones of the work, the use would not be an infringement. The limitations and exceptions system, on the other hand, shows a different perspective. In the EU's Svenson case, Rengifo indicates, the Court introduced a concept of implied consent regarding the uploading of copyrighted content without technical measures to control the use of such content. From there the Court indicated that an implied consent has been given that allows certain uses without prior and express consent. Such a decision can be very discussable, as this author mentions, but it also indicates the need for certain flexibilization on the copyright system. A more restricted system seems to exist under the Andean Community. However, the limitations and exceptions are interpreted in a way in which the judge would need to define some open concepts derived from the three steps rule. Would be that opening enough space to work out some of the uses that the internet requires? That is a question to develop in further legislative or judicial progress of the discipline.

Collective management

On a previous chapter (chapter 9), the collective management organisations and their capability of fulfilling the objective of guarantee the benefit of authors were assessed towards the resale right in the EU. One of the main questions on that chapter was whether statutory collective management was the only option possible to accomplish such an objective. The answer was negative. This chapter faces a similar question but with a wider perspective. It is aimed to understand if the idea of statutory collective management collides with the exclusive rights characterising copyright. The author focuses on the French solution to this problem and highlights the dilemma that implies the existence of statutory limitations and exceptions for which collective management is required and the creation of schemes of statutory collective management and extended collective licenses. Most of the attention in the chapter is given to this last concern, for which the author presents a study of comparative analysis of several countries from the EU and outside. The author concludes that the real issue at stake is the achievement of copyright purpose, particularly in the protection of author's interests for which is important that in their decisions, judges are aware of the particularities of the collective management organisations and their licensing schemes. Whether an exclusive right might seem in practice transformed into a mere remuneration right or not, the important issue is if in the practice the available options in benefit of the general stakeholders is better or not.

Albanian copyright towards the EU

Recent members of the EU have the burden of joining their copyright legislation with the obligations from the EU law. Blerina Mullisi's study relates to Albanian copyright history and development and how it can be adapted to the reality this country faces nowadays. After experiencing changes from the socialist regime in charge until 1990, the country has joined most of the copyright treaties but it yet has to confront some issues that according to the author are required to fully complete the integration with the EU law. Those areas of further work are in the field of public policies towards cooperation of institutions related to copyright in the country, particularly those related to its enforcement. Increasing awareness among the population about these rights is also an important issue of public policy. It is suggested that introducing copyright within the education curricula would help with such an aim. Those two actions would improve the way Albania responds to the protection of copyright in benefit of its nationals and foreigns.

Vietnam's copyright

Two chapters of the book are dedicated to some particularities of Vietnam's copyright. One of these is the chapter related to the possible causes of infringement of copyright in that country. The Law from 2005, which renewed the IP laws from 1995, is one of the first tools to achieve a better protection for authors. The author of chapter 21 in this Research Handbook asserts such an idea and supports it by analysing the development and characteristics of the copyright laws of this country. After doing this, the author explores the legal mechanisms at hand in Vietnam to enforce copyright, including the protection of technological measures used for self-protection of copyright, the existence of civil remedies, and also criminal remedies. In conclusion, for the author, it is still required that Vietnam's government implement further legal measures to fulfil the commitments acquired with the WTO. As Mullisi has indicated above on the previous chapter related to Albania's copyright, one of the principal issues ahead for Vietnam's government face is to improve cooperation amongst the concerned entities related to copyright. In addition, the author also highlights the need for more efficient and capable judiciary even suggesting the creation of specialised courts on the matter.

Kien's Chapter 22 explores Vietnam's copyright law from a different perspective. It studies the possible transplants the copyright laws of that country have experienced during their development. For this purpose, it has studied and compared the Vietnam's history on copyright law and the reception of the French influence while the country was a colony. Reaching the conclusion that the transplant of author's rights laws has been a process of dialogue and adaptation of the law, and that Vietnam's copyright law is older, dating its first developments on 1864. The author thus argues to debunk that copyright is of a recent development for this country.

Conclusion

A research handbook must push the boundaries of the discipline towards future activities of research, and this book does that. As shown in the previous section, the book amounts on several concerns regarding copyright with proposals of different kind and sometimes even showing from one author to another the existing debates on fields such as communication to the public, collective management, orphan works and cultural heritage, and so on. Therefore, the reader will find a strong element from which a top research can be started.

Legal Issues Journal

editor@uklsa.co.uk
http://www.legalissuesjournal.com

www.ingramcontent.com/pod-product-compliance
Lightning Source LLC
LaVergne TN
LVHW022048200926
848481LV00003B/822